TOO NORMAL

Child Abuse in Jamaica

TOO NORMAL

Kemone S-G Brown

First published in 2018

Copyright © Tamarind Hill Press 2018

All rights reserved

The moral right of Kemone S-G Brown to be identified as the author of this work has been asserted in accordance with the Copyright, Designs and Patents Act of 1988

No part of this publication may be reproduced, stored in a retrievable system, or transmitted, in any form or by any means, electronic, mechanical, photocopying, recording, or otherwise, without the prior written permission of both the copyright owner and publisher of this book.

Based on true events

Names and identifying details have been changed to protect the privacy and dignity of the individuals.

ISBN: 978-1-64467-337-9

TAMARiND HiLL
.PRESS

Acknowledgement

This book would not have been possible without the men and women who courageously shared their stories with me. To them I extend a heartfelt thank you. I have witnessed the pain so many of you are still in. My hope is that by being open and honest about what you went through, you will touch lives and impact conversations around ridding the Jamaican society of child abuse. Thank you all so much for aiding a quick turn around time on this project. I am forever grateful.

To Alexa-Ray, I do not know how to thank you. You have been an integral part in this process putting up with the emotional ups and downs. Thanks for your continued support and commitment to everything that I do. I could not have completed this project without your support.

A special thank you to Dalton Harris for walking into my life through the TV screen and reminding me that there is still so much that I want to do. Thank you for being open and honest and speaking your truth no matter how hard it was. Jamaican men and women, who have faced similar challenges as you have in your young life, salute you. Thanks for starting the conversation so that others may contribute to it in the hope that we can effect change in our little island. Your bravery and courage have given others the strength to find their own voice. Thank you.

Dedicated to boys and girls everywhere who are in this very moment being robbed of their childhood. Try to tell someone and keep shouting until someone listens and take accountability. Every child deserves a childhood; a happy one.

Epilogue

I'm sitting on my sofa in the living room watching X Factor when Dalton Harris came on screen. Looking into his eyes I could see a deep sadness in him. He didn't even speak yet when I turned around to the person I was watching with and said "he's so sad, he's in so much pain." I felt a deep sadness for him because I could see that he was troubled in a way that wasn't his fault. I remember asking a lot of questions. Why is he alone? What happened to him?

As the weeks went by and he began to open up about his life and what he'd been through, I felt for him. I wished with everything in me that he'd go on to win and find happiness somewhere. Learning that he was abused as a child made me realise why I'd recognised his sadness so quickly. Too often had I seen that same look in Jamaican adults and children; a burden they were carrying that wasn't their own to carry. I thought to myself, 'good for him, I hope this is a wakeup call for my fellow countrymen'. Boy was I about to be surprised.

Taking to social media, I saw the reaction of his mother and the Jamaican society at large. Surprisingly, so many people were attacking him for speaking out about child abuse. So many people thought he was bringing shame to his family and his country. I genuinely didn't understand how they hadn't seen it as a message; the wakeup call that it was. So many people called him a liar. In my heart I knew he wasn't lying. Like all these Jamaicans, I grew up in the society where children are constantly abused under the demise of 'discipline'. A society where parents and guardians beat children without any form of mercy or care for how it will affect them. A society where children are put down so much so that some of them start believing that they were worthless because they have heard it so many times. A society where children are given so much responsibilities that no child should take on.

It surprised me to see the Jamaican society's refusal to accept that in a lot of ways children are abused on a daily basis by their parents and those meant to guide and protect them. As has always been the case, the children were still being blamed, "I'm sure he was bad", "her mother didn't mean any harm", "the bible said not to spare the rod and spoil the child". When will children stop being blamed for adults' inability to control their anger; for taking out their frustrations on children; for burdening children with their own responsibilities? When will we be concerned about changing the outcome?

Every day promising children are robbed of their childhood, their happiness and their future. Abused children become affected adults. The majority doesn't manage to escape the effects of what they went through in their childhood. So many become adults who cry themselves to sleep at night still wondering what they did to their parents to have caused them to treat them that way. Many of them fail to have stable lives; they stay in abusive relationships and sometimes end up being killed by their abusers because they do not know any better.

Our shame shouldn't be the fact that Dalton spoke out about his abuse. The shame should be the wide acceptance of child abuse. The shame is in the fact that we see it as so normal; too normal. Instead of being ashamed we should pool together to see what needs to be done to enable parents and guardians to do better; raise a happier generation plagued with less traumatised adults. It is not enough to say that 'I got beaten and it didn't kill me', or 'I got beaten and I turned out well'. Some of us aren't strong enough and why should children be broken down at all? As black people we have fought so hard to get away from slavery; the beatings, being without food as a form of punishment, the constant inhumane treatment. Why are these treatments now good enough for our children?

Ten people have shared their stories with me and through this book you. I have witnessed the pain these people are still in. So many of them still cry when they talk about what they've been through. It's time for change. It's time to pool together and strive for better as a people and as a nation. These stories aren't fun and enjoyable; most of them are toned down because some of the things done to some of these contributors were too vile to write about. How many more children must go through this before we realise how damaging it is?

It's not discipline. It's not something they'll get over in time. It's child abuse that plagues their lives and our society. It needs to end.

Injustice against any human being is injustice against humankind

Cherish

There is no place in my life for my mother. As horrible as that might sound it is unfortunately my reality. Surely I would help her if I saw her on the street in need of food or water for the simple fact that she's another human being. Outside of that, there is nothing between us and there will never be. I don't resent her, and I have forgiven her, but I have learned the hard way that there is nothing between us and it was either I let go or forever have her ruin my life. I'm 29 years old and for 27 of those years my mother and my sisters were the bane of my existence, literally. If you don't believe that a mother can hate her own child, you are very wrong. The woman hates me. To be frank, I don't think she even loves herself which is sad. Unfortunately, it is no longer my concern whether she loves herself or not. I wake up every day now grateful that she gave me life but there really is nothing else. I have tried having a relationship with her. I have tried everything I possibly can. I've had enough.

My mother had six daughters before me. The man she was with before my *father* was a fair skinned man, who according to her gave her the best-looking daughters. My sisters are light skinned with curly hair. Me on the other hand; I'm 'black like tar' as they would all point out every chance they got. Other than my sister before me, I now have nothing to do with them.

I never met my *father*. No matter how much I beg her to be honest with me and at least tell me his name she has refused. That is just one of the ways in which she tortures me. I had a conversation with her years ago and explained to her that I wouldn't care if he'd raped her and she wanted me to have nothing to do with him, I just wanted to know; but she refused to tell me. In one of the neighbourhoods that we lived, a lady in passing said I looked just like my father. I was too young to understand enough to ask her more and no man has ever claimed me as their own.

My sisters and my mother made and continued to make my life a living hell until I broke away from them completely two years ago. They were all close in age. I was the youngest at home and my sister before me was four years older.

"Stop pushing me," I remember my little voice; crying and trying to get them to stop pushing me around.

They laughed as they stood in a circle pushing me from one to the other over and over and over again. When I fell from a push, another of my sisters would pick me up then push me to another one in the circle, who'd push me to another. This game was mild compared to the many other's they played. One of their favourites was hide and seek. One of them would pretend we were hiding together then would put me in one of the drawers on the chest of drawer and leave me there. It would be dark, so I couldn't see anything. I wouldn't be able to move my limbs. After a long while no one would come to find me, and I'd have to cry long and hard before anyone let me out.

One day my sister was eating a mango and I asked for some, I wasn't even five yet. At first, she refused to give me the mango then she got up from the step, walked over to the dog mess in the yard and dropped the mango then used her foot to rub it in the mess. She called me over to get the mango. When I wouldn't, she went into the house to get a black plastic bag, took up the mango walked over to me and rubbed it in my face. I was screaming when one of my other sisters came outside, saw what she was doing, and instead of telling her to stop she got into a fit of laughter. I was so humiliated. I told my mother who did nothing.

As I started to get older, I got lonely. It was evident I was an outcast. They never played with me or anything like that. When my sister before me, Destiny, would try to do anything nice for me, the others would stop her. Sometimes she would hide and give me something to eat or read to me while the others were still at school but whenever they were around, she avoided me like the plague. I remembered even at school I was afraid to trust other kids or make friends because I couldn't imagine them being genuinely nice or would be nice to me if other people were looking. I had a very lonely childhood.

I remember coming home with my report card, so excited because I had gotten all A's. I was only in grade one. I was so proud of myself. I came running into the yard to show them and my eldest sister caught me running and took the paper from me.

"What is this?"

"My report. I'm first! Teacher says I'll get a present."

"Present for what?" She hissed her teeth then began ripping the paper to shreds.

I jumped trying to get the paper away from her hand, but she held it too high. When she was done, the paper was all over the ground in bits. I looked around feeling helpless and empty. She'd ruined my day. She was the worst one amongst them - my eldest sister. She was second to my mother: the more miserable they could make my life the better their life was. I didn't tell anyone about my report card that day or any subsequent ones. No one had even checked why I was crying.

The Friday of that week, I got a doll and a full page of gold stars in my book from my teacher. I hid the doll in my bag and hid my bag under the bed when I got home. I wanted to play with the doll so bad because I'd never had one for myself. I was so excited but I knew that if they saw it I would lose it. While everyone slept the Saturday morning, I sneaked under the bed and played with the doll inside my school bag; too scared to take it out. When I heard a shift on the bed I stayed still until it stopped then came out from under the bed. One of my sisters were awake and asked why I was under the bed. She got up from the bed and looked under the bed but only saw my bag, the doll was still hiding away inside.

"Why were you under the bed?"

"Nothing, just looking for something."

"Looking for what?"

"Nothing."

"Don't go under the bed," she pushed me in my forehead with her finger.

"Okay."

The following day they found the doll and took it out to the front yard to burn it while I cried and begged them not to. My eldest sister told me to stop crying or she'd burn me in the fire too.

From as early as I could remember my mother was beating me. The strange thing though was how different she'd beat me compared to how she'd beat my sisters. To beat them she'd send them to get the belt and ask them to hold out their hands, which would be the only place she'd hit them. She was very protective of their skin and I do think this contributed to the way she avoided hitting them anywhere but in their hands. That added to the fact that she actually liked them and didn't like me.

One morning I was getting ready for school. I was really young; I was in pre-school. I bathed myself but wanted to use the toilet after I'd put my uniform on. When I walked past my mother, she must've smelled me.

"Why do you smell like that? You used the toilet?"

"Yes mommy."

"You wiped your bottom?"

"Yes mommy."

"Come here you smell like shit."

I walked over to her feeling shy and exposed.

"This damn little girl shit on her damn uniform!" she started beating me on my bum with her hand. Her hand touched the faeces on my uniform and it made her mad. "Look now, the damn shit is on my hand. This damn little girl." My mother leaned back in the sofa and kicked me in my stomach. I fell back on the coffee table and the glass shattered. My mother got up and picked me up by my neck and slammed me down on the floor on my back. "One of you come get this little girl before I end up killing her."

One of my sisters came to get me. She took me into the bathroom, put me inside the shower and turned on the tap then left. I was so young, but I remember thinking how cruel they all were. I had to bathe and dress myself for school and I was only four or five. I didn't do a good job at cleaning up myself and instead of helping me my mother had beaten me.

By the age of five I was responsible for making runs to the shop. According to my mother, I was the smart one and the only one who would remember all the things to get. I didn't see the logic from that very young age because it was a simple fix, write a list and they'd be able to tell the shopkeeper what they wanted. It was a pattern being developed. Very soon, I was going to be the only one who could do a lot of things to please her.

Coming home from school one afternoon, I believe I was in the second grade, I found my mother waiting outside with a piece of board much longer than her arm in hand.

"Good afternoon mommy," I said gayly.

"Cherish, why didn't you wash the dishes this morning?"

"Uhm, I woke up late mommy. I'm going to wash them now."

"You like when I beat you, don't you?"

"No mommy, I will wash them now."

"Put down your bag and come here."

I was shaking, I knew I was in for it. I couldn't walk slowly enough to put my bag inside. I wished that time would stop and I could wash the dishes so my mother would forget about beating me.

"Cherish! Don't let me have to call you again!"

I started shaking, literally. "I'm coming mommy." I pleaded with my legs to walk faster. "Mommy, I'm going to wash the dishes now."

"Don't play with me. Come here."

My legs went dead again. I was always afraid of being beaten. I didn't walk fast enough so my mother got up from the step and came to collar me by my uniform blouse on the veranda. She raised the piece of board and I covered my eyes before it hit me on my thigh. My mother kept beating me until a nail in the board got stuck into my left bum cheek. It took her a while to pull it out and as soon as it was, she continued beating me.

My mother never saw to the wound. It was a lady down the road who'd always talk to me on my way to the shop who burned green banana and dressed it. I stopped by her house every morning before school and she dressed the wound until it was healed. That lady was a blessing in my life. For the years that we lived in the neighbourhood, she'd help me out with food, taxi fare, anything. Once she even gave me a pair of shoes for school. I was wearing an old tattered pair of shoes which was two sizes too small for my feet. Then one morning when I was passing for school, she called me over and gave me a pair of brand-new shoes. I was in the third grade by then and hadn't had a pair of new shoes in forever: I was more than over joyed. She kept my old shoes at her house while I went to school, which I would change back into on my way home. She was a really kind lady. I was sad to move away from that neighbourhood because I was leaving behind the only person who consistently showed me any form of kindness.

One morning my mother told me to wash the dishes. I was running late and all my sisters were already gone. It was one of my sister's turn to do them the night before and as usual she'd refused to do them. In the night I was tempted to wash them because I knew it would fall back on me, but I refused because that happened almost every evening. My mother said we would take turns with different chores but that was only in theory. It was always my turn to do everything.

"Mommy it was Barbara's turn to do the dishes. It's not fair that I should always do their chores."

"Wash them up and don't let me have to tell you again."

All I could think of was that my shoes were blinding me and I needed to hurry to meet up with Ms Lesley before she left for work so I could change them. I also needed to rush so I wasn't late. I quickly washed the plates, spoons and cups. The rice had burnt the night before so there was no way I could wash the pot before soaking it. I filled it up with water and left it on the side of the sink. I washed my hands and grabbed my bookbag ready to go. I was already through the gate.

"Cherish! Come here."

"Mommy I'm going to be late." I reluctantly came back into the yard.

"Come here and stop talking back to me."

I knew this trick. My mother didn't give me money for school: no taxi fare or anything. She was going to try everything to hold me back from school. As usual I'd prepared my mind to be quick. The worse case scenario, in my mind, was that I'd miss Ms Lesley, not have taxi fare and have to wear the undersized shoes all the way to school. I'd most likely have to take it off and walk barefooted to save myself from the pain. I'd simply just rush through any chore she'd give me real fast.

"Why didn't you wash the rice pot? Wash it and scour it too."

"But mommy, they didn't soak it. The rice can't come out."

"Then wait for it to come out then."

"But mommy I have to go to school."

"Stop annoying me and don't make me angry."

I went to wash the pot, though I knew it was impossible at the time. I used a spoon to dig the burnt rice stuck to it but couldn't get rid of most of it. I was only eight and underfed so I could hardly lift the pot, let alone dig the rice out.

"Mommy, I can't get the rice out. I'll wash it when I get home."

My mother stepped pass me outside the back door, walked over to the sink, took up the rice pot filled with water and poured it on my head. I was soaked from head to toe. Even my bookbag and books got wet. "Wash the damn pot and don't tell me foolishness!" She dropped the pot on the ground and went back inside.

I was so shocked that she'd done that. It was the first time she'd done it but it wouldn't have been her last. It was one of her tactics used to stop me from school. She'd throw the soap water she washed clothes in, the dishwashing water and even once poured urine from her chamber pot on me in my uniform. I'd still go to school the same way I had done that morning. When Miss Lesley saw me that morning, she was shocked. I could tell she wanted to cry.

"You won't be a child forever, Cherish. Just be strong and keep God close. One day you'll get away."

"God doesn't love me Ms Lesley, that's why he makes my mother treat me like this."

"Don't ever say a thing like that. Don't let the devil control your mind. You have to be strong."

"I just want to go to school."

"Then you'll go to school and make the best of it. Put God first and you will keep doing well in school and you can make something of yourself and have your own life. You won't stay young forever. Always remember that and keep God right by your side."

"Okay Ms Lesley."

She rinsed my uniform and ironed it dry. I changed into the shoes she'd gotten me and she walked with me to the shop to buy me a note book to take to school, then we took a taxi together. She kept my bag at her house on the line to dry. I was so late, she told the teacher she was my aunt and it was her fault I was late. I suppose she'd felt that I couldn't handle more punishment that morning.

Throughout the entire day my mind was occupied by what my mother had done. I was worried about what she'd do when I got home. I'd left without saying anything to her. Instead of telling her once more that I couldn't wash the pot I decided to just leave as soon as she was in the house. I couldn't play or talk to anyone. Ms Lesley had given me money to buy lunch but I couldn't even think about eating. I remember just wishing she'd been my mother and that I could live with her. She was such a sweet person and she didn't have children of her own. As young as I was, I thought how strange God was. My mother had eight children and I was one too many; the one I'm sure she never wanted. Yet there was this very nice lady who was the sweetest kindest person I know, and she didn't have children.

When school ended, I didn't want to go home but I knew I had to. I stopped by Ms Lesley's house but she wasn't home yet. I had to wait for her. I saw one of my sisters coming up the street and hid in the bushes until she passed.

If she saw me there, she would tell my mother and I was sure they'd find a way to make sure I couldn't go there again. I'd taken so many precautions to hide the fact that Ms Lesley was helping me. Ms Lesley came home and packed my books back into my bag and I changed back into my old shoes. She showed me the Cinderella story book she bought for me and said she'd let me read it when I came by. We both knew that I couldn't take it home. I walked home with glee. I couldn't wait to go back to read the book. I'd never had a story book before. The only time I'd seen one was when I was much younger. My sister Destiny had one that I wasn't allowed to touch. Now I had my own book. I couldn't take it home but it was in a safe place and I could read it on my way home from school. I was elated.

When I got home, my mother wasn't in the house. It was her day off so she should have been there but she wasn't. Before taking off my uniform I ran around the back to wash the pot which was still soaking. I scoured it too and rinsed it, dried it then put it back into the cupboard. I was hoping she hadn't realised that I hadn't done it this morning.

My mother came home not long after and didn't mention anything about the pot. I was relieved. My eldest sister who was in college called everyone into the living room to watch TV with her. When I trailed behind them, she told me to go back into the bedroom I slept in. This was common, so I didn't mind too much. I was used to being cast aside and left out of everything. I felt left out but there was not much I could do about it. In the room there was nothing to do. I'd already done my homework, so I took out a book I'd seen one of my older sisters with. It was a Social Studies book which had poems from Ms Lou in it. I was immersed in the book when my sister came to see what I was doing.

"Blackie-best, why are you so quiet? What are you doing in here?"

I was frightened, I tried to hide the book next to me. "Nothing."

"What do you mean nothing? Let me see what you're hiding."

"I'm not hiding anything."

"Let me see," she grabbed the book from me. "Fay, come here. Blackie have your book."

"What, which book?"

"This," she handed her the book.

"Don't touch my things man," she slapped me with the book across my face. "I don't want your tar to rub off on anything for me."

"Sorry," I said, filled with shame.

"Sit on the floor," Fay instructed.

"Exactly, I don't know why she needs to rub herself on things other people have to touch." Esme added with contempt. "Move," she kicked me.

"Sorry," I said again.

The two of them left the room and I sat still where they'd left me. I didn't want them to come back in and get angry for something else. Not long after, my mother called me. It was dinner time.

"Why didn't you wash the pot?"

"I washed it mommy." I could see the pot on the fire.

"So you decided to wash it when you felt like it?"

"No mommy."

"Don't interrupt me. Being that you washed the pot when you felt like washing it. I'll also feed you when I feel like it. Tonight I don't feel like giving you any dinner. Sit in the corner over there and face me." She pointed to the corner next to the single seated sofa behind the front door.

I struggled to get into the corner. I had to shift the sofa a bit. I sat down on the floor and buried my face between my raised knees.

"Hey, lift up your head and look at me. Watch me eat."

"Hahahaha, you should give her some bottle covers to kneel down on." Esme added.

The others laughed in unison.

"She's lucky I don't have," my mother replied.

"I'll pick some up off the road tomorrow and bring home for you. You need some in the house." Fay added.

"Blackie-best when I'm done eating you can eat my bones okay." She teased.

As soon as they were done eating, I had to wash the dishes. I'd hoped there'd be some scrapings in the bottom of the pots but I wasn't lucky enough. I was so hungry but all that was left on their plates were chewed up bones. Outside in the dark I washed the dishes slowly in hope that they'd all be sleeping by the time I was finished. Unfortunately, when I went inside with the washed dishes, they were all still wide awake, watching TV.

"Cherish, I don't see the point of you always crying to go to school. There really is no point of you going. You don't need to pass English or Maths to wash people's clothes or clean their houses. That's all you'll amount to anyway."

I continued crying because I wanted to go to school and even harder because of what she'd said. Esme was working now and my mother refused to give me money to buy my art stuff so I'd asked her. I don't know what had even possessed me to ask her for help.

"It's okay Esme. Sorry I asked."

"You mustn't learn to beg either."

"Sorry Esme."

It was my second week in high school. I was the first and only one at home to pass for a top traditional high school and my sisters were not happy. Over the summer they told me how I'd better not bother to go because I wasn't going to use the knowledge anyway. They teased me about how I was too black to wear the uniform and how the school was only for light skinned, rich kids. They told me I'd not fit in so it was pointless going. They told me horror stories about how other kids were treated there. Nothing they told me was worse than how I was being treated at home and I wasn't stupid enough to believe them. It dawned on me that they were simply jealous.

"Look at your hair. It looks like coconut brush. And look at your nose. Oh my god, Cherish I just realised now. You know you have a Bell-pepper shaped nose." Fay laughed, "yes, I finally see it now."

"And what do you have?"

"Who do you think you're talking to? Don't try me, I'll make you eat your words."

"Sorry."

"Damn right you're sorry. Come clean my toes, you need to practise. When somebody finally hires you as a helper it will be good that you can provide additional services. You need to learn."

"The water is still boiling."

"Turn up the fire and hurry it up, remember you still have the bathroom to clean and you need to put the white clothes to soak so you can wash them tomorrow."

"Okay."

Every week over the summer I had to give Fay a pedicure. She had a problem with her feet that caused the skin to be extremely dry and constantly shed. My mother would give her money to go get her feet done but she'd pocket the money and let me do them. I didn't see the point of telling my mother because she'd never stopped them from doing anything. If I'd stood up for myself against one of them she'd beat me instead. I was not supposed to be disobedient to my elder sisters. If they said jump, I wasn't even supposed to ask how high; I was supposed to jump.

One afternoon in the seventh grade, I came home to find the sink full of dishes to wash. The night before I wasn't given any dinner so I decided I wouldn't wash them. I was more outraged in the morning, as they all had breakfast and refused to give me any. I'd left the house in anger. It was regular now for them not to give me any dinner, breakfast, lunch money; nothing. Then they expected me to carry on doing chores. No one knew how I ate, and no one cared. There was a church close to my school that served breakfast. They served breakfast on Tuesday and Thursday mornings, so I'd leave early enough to make sure I'd catch it. They often served fried dumplings for breakfast and I'd eat one and save the other three and make them last in between visits. I'd hide them in foil in the pockets of my bag. One Monday afternoon one of my friends went into the pocket looking for a pen and found my stash; the last one from the batch I'd been keeping from the Thursday before. It was going off, as they often did. She asked about it and I told her I'd forgotten it in there. She took it out and threw it in the bin. I died inside knowing that I'd have to wait for the following morning to go to the church. Tina was my closest friend but she never knew my circumstances. At lunch time I'd go to a club meeting. I'd joined every single club there was to make sure I'd not have to be around her at lunch time. She was not into that kind of stuff as she'd usually say so I was safe. Sometimes I'd steal food at home; but it was ever so little as I'd always tried to make sure it wasn't obvious that I'd stolen it. When I think about it I realise how sick and evil my family was. It didn't bother them one bit that I didn't have food. I was so skinny you could see the bones protruding in different places.

It got to the point that I'd even go through the market and pick up whatever I could salvage from the piles of discarded vegetables and fruits the sellers accumulated. I remember once there was a man who saw me and called me over to give me a piece of the watermelon he was selling. I devoured it so fast he gave me a second piece.

I soon started to rebel. I decided that I wasn't going to keep working like a horse with no food. When I came home to find the dishes still piled up I laughed to myself. I changed into a red dress I had, it was one of my only two options. My only other piece of clothing outside of the two suits of uniforms I had was a green dress Destiny had given to me. The red dress was so tattered I had sewn it in places so many times to keep it together. It was so short you could see everything if I bent slightly forward. I went outside and sat with my books, putting the ones I wasn't using on my lap to hide my thighs. I buried my head in my book doing my homework.

"Cherish!" Esme, called out.

I didn't answer because I knew exactly why she was calling me and I was determined not to wash them. I started packing up my books, knowing full well she was coming out any minute to attack me. I was still packing them up when she came outside on the veranda.

"Come wash up the dishes."

"I didn't use any dishes so I won't wash them."

"You're too funny and I'm not in for your jokes right now. Come wash up the dishes and don't let me have to come out there."

"It's fine you can come because I'm not washing them."

"One of you guys come out here and tell this little black gal not to play with me. I need to cook so she needs to come wash up the dishes."

"Whose turn is it to wash them up though," Destiny questioned.

"Don't get involved!" she shouted at Destiny. "It's her turn to wash them up, it's always her turn."

"You guys can kill me today, but I won't wash them."

In the blink of an eye I was being jumped by my sisters. I was being kicked all over my body. They kept kicking and I shielded my face with my hands.

"Stop and let her come wash up the dishes," Esme ordered the others.

"I'm not washing them up!" I said with all my might.

"This fucking gal think I'm playing with her. Arianna bring me the big metal spoon." She left and returned with the spoon and Esme used it to beat me all over my body. Even with all the beating I was determined I wasn't going to wash them. When she turned her back, I ran to the front of the yard close to the gate and climbed as fast as I could to the top of the mango tree. I knew there was no way any of them would come up there. I stayed in the tree until my mother came home. She demanded that I come down and when I didn't, she began throwing rocks at me. One of them knocked me in my face, barely missing my eye causing a wound just below my left brow. The blood streamed down my face making it impossible for me to see. My mother continued throwing stones at me. I could hardly see from my right eye and missed my footing, causing me to fall on another branch beneath me, hitting my vagina hard on the branch. My sister pulled me by my leg and I fell out of the tree on my back. My mother sat on me, punching me in my face repeatedly then ordered me to wash up the dishes. I had to wash them.

My mother never treated me well. When it came time to do my CXC exams, my mother refused to pay the fees. I told the guidance counsellor at school and the school paid the difference for the subjects that weren't covered by the bank and the government. I finished high school with 1s in all my subjects and was pleased that I could make everyone who had helped me proud.

In my final year, I finally ran away one day after my mother had set fire to my hair. My hair was coarse and hard to comb. I wasn't particularly good at combing it so unless one of the girls at school braided it for me, I'd end up looking like a mad woman most days. In the mornings I'd struggle to get the comb through it. I asked her whether she could relax it the way she'd done all the other's hair and she refused. When I tried explaining to her that teachers were complaining about the state of my hair she literally just got up, went for the box of matches, struck one and threw it in my afro. I ran around the house like a headless chicken trying to put it out before it dawned on me to put my head under the running tap. All my sisters and my mother laughed about it all afternoon and evening. They found it funny that they could smell my hair burning. Luckily for me the fire didn't burn to the skin.

The same night while they slept, I climbed out the window taking all my worldly belongings which were; my one suit of uniform for school, an old uniform dress I now wore at home, the two extra panties I had, all my school books and my pair of socks and shoes. I stole one of my sister's slippers, a t-shirt and a skirt. I didn't even have a tooth brush. I used to use my panty to bathe and 'brush' my teeth. It was dark outside, and I was scared to death, but I had had enough. It took days for the burning hair smell to go, even after balding my head entirely.

I was homeless for weeks. I would sneak into someone's yard early in the morning to use their outside pipe to wash myself. In the nights I'd wonder through neighbourhoods until I could find a tree to sleep in. I didn't want to tell anyone what was going on because I was too ashamed. I felt disregarded and thought about how happy they were to have woken up and found me finally gone and out of their lives. No one turned up at school to look for me. There were no missing girl reports, nothing. No one cared.

One evening after school my friend Tina asked whether I wanted to come over to her house. All the other times I'd said no but this time I didn't have to worry I'd be beaten for getting home late or anything for that matter, so I took her up on her offer. I pretended to call my mother from their house phone the evening to ask my mother if I could stay over. I told Mrs Wilson my mother had given me permission to sleep over. It was so nice to be given a hot meal and a warm bed to sleep in.

I asked to go home with Tina again the following evening but it was Friday and her family were going out of town for the weekend so she said it wasn't possible. I was waiting with her outside the school gate for her mother to come. When her mother pulled up, she called me over.

"Hi Cherish," she said in her usual calm voice.

"Hello Mrs Wilson."

"How was school?"

"It was okay as usual Mrs Wilson. How was your day?"

"It was good, thanks. Tina you never ask how my day was," she smirked, "you should let a little of Cherish rub off on you." She smiled at me. "Did Tina tell you we are going to her grandparents for the weekend? Do you want to come with us?"

"Uhm," I paused.

"Aw mom can she? Yes yes come Cherish. Please please please please please please please. Then we can study together on Sunday when we get back."

"You can call your mother to ask her. I can wait."

I took the phone and pretended to call my mother. Returning to the car, I handed her the phone and told her my mother said I could go.

"Do you want," she stopped herself. "Oh, never mind. How about we go for a little retail therapy so us girls can have something new for the weekend."

"No we don't have to." I said.

"Yes we have to," Tina added quickly. "Mom remember you promised to buy me a new pair of white Adidas. Can we get them today?"

"Come on, I insist. Let's go shopping."

I didn't know then, but Mrs Wilson was on the PTA committee and was one of the parents who had contributed to help pay for my CXC exams. Apparently, the school had gone to my house on two separate occasions to speak with my mother who was unable to present me both times. She knew I wasn't living there. The Monday morning Mrs Wilson came into the guest bedroom where I was sleeping. I was already dressed for school waiting for the house to come alive. I was so used to waking up early, I couldn't sleep past 5am.

"Cherish, where do you stay when you're not here?"

"What do you mean Mrs Wilson? I stay at home."

"Okay, and do you like staying at home?"

I nodded in agreement. I could tell she didn't know how to bring it up but it was obvious she knew more than she was letting on.

"Wouldn't you like to stay here with us? You and Tina could study together."

"No Mrs Wilson, it's okay. I don't want to bother you."

"You're not a bother, we all like having you here. You could keep this room and no one would bother you."

I began to cry, "I can't stay here."

"I didn't mean to make you cry Cherish, I'm sorry. We'll leave it alone for now. Have a think then if you want, you can come home with Tina today. Wash your face then come down. I'll go prepare breakfast." She leaned in to hug me but it startled me. "Oh sorry, I apologise." She left the room.

I sat on the bed and cried uncontrollably. I wanted so bad to accept her kindness so I could have a place to stay and food to eat, but all I could think of was the shame. What would she have really thought if I was just there with her; a child whose mother didn't know where she was and wasn't out looking for her? I cried more out of shame and embarrassment more than anything else. When I finally made it down to breakfast I couldn't eat. I sat at the breakfast table fighting back tears. Seeing the way they interacted with each other was overwhelming. I felt happy for Tina and Timothy that they were so blessed to have the parents they had. It made me realise just how Tina could afford to be friends with me, even though we were nothing alike. I think the kindness in her knew I needed the kindness and she gave that to me.

Mrs Wilson took out money for all three of us. I remember looking down at the $500 bill thinking how crazy it was to have so much money. I'd never had this much money for myself and worse just for food. In the back of my mind I reminded myself that I'd have to make it last.

During lunch, I was called to the principal's office. Inside the office my principal was waiting with the guidance counsellor and Mrs Wilson. They told me they knew I wasn't living at home and Mrs Wilson explained that she'd noticed that I had clothes in my school bag. The point was that they weren't sure what was going on but it was obvious that I needed help and Mrs Wilson and her husband were willing to take me in and look after me. The whole time I couldn't speak, I just sat there and cried. This time when Mrs Wilson hugged me I wasn't frightened. It reminded me of Ms Lesley. I remember hugging her back, feeling safe and relieved.

I lived with them until Tina and I went off to University together and they rented an apartment for us. They are still my family and Tina and I are closer than can be. Even today, although she's recently married, we are literally inseparable. When the nights are hard to get through, Tina is available on the other end of the phone or willing to come over to help me get through it.

My first attempt at reconnecting with my mother was a few weeks before my high school graduation. I'd gone to invite her and she flat out refused. I remember how surprised she looked to see me well dressed. She looked me over a few times. She said she had no reason for coming to my graduation but I told her the date, time and venue and told her it would be nice if she could just show up so I'm not the only child without family there. Graduation came and I searched the crowd for her but she never showed.

While going to college, I had a cell phone which Mr and Mrs Wilson had gotten me. Every week without fail I'd call the house and try to speak to whoever would answer the phone. More times than often they'd just hang up when they realised it was me. Then one day I called my mother who was crying on the other end of the phone. Everyone had now moved out of the house to live their own lives. She said she was lonely; that no one had any time for her.

The following week I went by the house to check on her, to see how she was doing. I hadn't seen her in almost two years. She looked different. She looked sad. She wasn't her usual upbeat self. The house was also messy; not particularly dirty but it was obvious that it hadn't been given a proper clean in a long while. I decided to clean and cook for her. I remember thinking how strange it was for her to talk to me like I existed. She asked me about my life and where I was living but I didn't answer her truthfully. I didn't lie either, I just told her I was okay and getting by.

For the rest of the time that I was still around, which was about four or so months, I continued to visit her once per week to help her clean and take care of the house. Then the day before I went off to University, Mrs Wilson drove me to say my goodbyes. Turning up at the house it was evident something was happening.

A few people were sitting on the veranda, most of them I didn't know. I said good evening and went inside to find my mother.

"What is this? Esme, come quick. Look who is standing in our house."

"Who?" Esme asked without presenting herself.

"Fay, I don't want any problems. I'm just here to see mommy."

"Hey don't say that for anyone to hear. I don't want anyone to know I'm related to you." She stepped forward and whispered.

"I can't believe my eyes. Blackie-best, what are you doing here? Fay she look decent though." Esme flipped my blouse. "Who bought you clothes?"

"I'm just here to see mommy."

"Don't say that out of your mouth again," Fay slapped me across my face.

I stood looking at her thinking of all the ways they'd tormented me, made my life a living hell. All I could see was blackness around me and Fay standing right in front of me. I slapped her first then just started punching her. Esme started pulling me and I turned to punch her too.

"Hey, all three of you stop it!" my mother shouted. "Cherish, get out of my house now!" she pointed to the door.

The entire ride home I never said a word to Mrs Wilson. It wasn't until more recently that I finally told Tina what had happened that day.

Over the years I made several attempts to reconnect with my family. My mother would pretend she'd accepted me into her life when she was all alone but as soon as one of her prized possessions gave her an ounce of attention, she'd cast me aside like garbage.

When I was 26, Destiny sought me out. When she found me, I hadn't spoken to my mother for almost six months after she'd used a teapot to bash me over the head while I was at her house arguing with Ariana. She had come over to my mother's and found me cooking for her. She told me to leave and I ignored her so she came into the kitchen to drag me out. I fought back. My mother came in and took up the teapot off the stove and bashed me in the back of my head and told me to 'leave her daughter'. That said a lot to me. She really didn't see me as a part of her. I left her house and blocked her landline and cell number from my phone. There was no way for her to get in touch with me.

Destiny called telling me my mother was in the hospital. She was diagnosed with diabetes. On the same phone call Destiny took the opportunity to apologise for everything she'd ever done to me and asked for my forgiveness. I knew she didn't have a choice, otherwise she'd have possibly been in the same position as me so I had nothing to hold against her. I showed up at the hospital to help Destiny with my mother. None of the others came around for months, she only had the two of us but mainly me as Destiny was almost always busy with her children. One day I was there with my mother when my sister Barbara came over. I never liked a bone in her from day one. She was sneaky and evil. Unlike Esme who would let you know straight up that she didn't like you, Barbara would always go about it in a sneaky evil vindictive way. I was used to her though but not enough to realise what was in store for me.

"Hi Cherish."

"Hi." I said with no regard for her whatsoever.

"Why are you answering me like that though. You need to let things stay in the past and try to move on. We are all adults now."

"You were an adult when you did a lot of the things you did to me. You weren't a child."

"Cherish life is too short, grow up."

"Grow up? Grow up? Didn't you think you needed to grow up when you were treating me like shit? Didn't you think you all needed to grow up when I would have to wash all your clothes, clean the house top to bottom and do anything else you guys wanted? Huh, are you grown up? Didn't you think you all should grow up when you ganged me last year?"

"Alright alright woe is you. Always wanting people to be sorry for you. Every family have rivalry, especially sisters. It's life, get over yourself. You're not special. All of a sudden you have your big job you think everyone should throw themselves at your mercy. You're still nobody Cherish. You will always be nobody."

"Yup, there goes the grown up."

"I didn't mean that, sorry."

"Wow I didn't know that you knew that word," I clapped sarcastically.

"Cherish I'm not trying to argue with you. We need to try to get along. Anyone of us can die any time, I don't want to go to my grave with any burden on my heart or with anyone hating me. Let's just let the past stay in the past and start afresh. You're my little sister and I'm here for you."

The following week for my birthday Barbara called to wish me a happy birthday. I didn't even know that any of them knew my birthday because none of them had ever wished me or even acknowledged the day. She wanted to meet up for drinks but as was now tradition, I was at Mr and Mrs Wilson's with the rest of the family celebrating. I promised to meet up with her over the weekend.

It seemed like they were making an effort sending me text messages during the week and calling every now and then. They all had children. Other than Destiny's three children, I'd never met any of them. Gina was pregnant the same year I ran away but I'd never met the baby. I'd tell Tina about their efforts every time we talked, and she'd remind me to not get my hopes up. She'd witnessed every failed attempt to make things right with them.

Barbara called me out of the blue one Sunday afternoon to borrow $50,000. I was shocked. I couldn't imagine why she'd think that I'd have that kind of money on hand to lend to her. I explained that I didn't have it and she was obviously not pleased. Not long after she'd hung up a call came in from Esme who was pleading with me to give Barbara the money. I explained to her that I didn't have that kind of money on hand as I'd explained to her already. Suddenly, Arianna came on the phone mad; telling me how they were going to burn down my house and how I couldn't walk on the street without one of them hurting me. I hung up in the middle of her rant. The next phone call was my mother. She quarrelled for about three good minutes before I could get a word in. Then I'm not sure what had taken me over but what she said next would put an end to anything that could have been between us.

"You're too ungrateful......"

"What did you just say to me mommy?"

She continued quarrelling but I wasn't going to let it go. "Let me tell you something and God knows after today I want nothing to do with you. Ungrateful? Ungrateful to who and for what? What did any of you ever do for me? How have you contributed to my life? Ungrateful? You and all your children are a bunch of wicked evil people. None of you care about me, not one. It's obvious now why everyone is nice all of a sudden. Everyone wants to see what they can get. But let me make it clear, I have nothing to give to any of you. Who is ungrateful?" I was struggling to catch my breath. "I still have nightmares of the things all of you did to me. What kind of mother wakes up and not see her child but don't even report them missing? How am I ungrateful? I should thank you and them for all the wicked things you did to me? You want me thank you for giving me life? Well you know what mommy, thanks. Thanks for bringing me into the world and thanks for everything all of you did to me. Don't ever call my phone again."

I hung up my phone and that was the last time I spoke with any of them.

Harriet

"The thing is mommy doesn't think she's doing anything wrong. You can't allow it to break you."

"How can I not allow it to break me? I'm already broken. Don't come to me with this bullshit about her not thinking she's doing anything wrong. She's not a baby. She knows she's an evil bitch!"

"Hey, please lower your voice because if she hears you it's only going to make things worse. God knows I can't take anymore today. I'm sure you can't either."

"Don't tell me to shut up. I want her to hear me. She wants to kill me, and I want her to. I'm tired of living like this! I'm tired of all this shit!"

"I'm not telling you to shut up. You know what. You can stay here and shout all you want. You might get what you want. She might come in and kill you for real.

"Let her come kill me. I'll be better off dead!"

"Harriet, I'm going outside."

"Whatever."

Susanna left the room and Harriet got up from the bed and started packing. She couldn't ignore the stinging pain in her skin all over her body. Her right eye was swollen shut. The place in her head where her mother had ripped the hair from was aching and throbbing. As she put her clothes in the bag, she cried. In her mind she wanted to die right then and there. She was only thirteen and had tried taking her life so many times before that they knew her well at the hospital. Her sister was much more resilient. She was the older of the two and had been going through it longer; she'd built up somewhat of a thick skin. She accepted that this was her mother and that she couldn't really change it. It was better than her other options. Her father was a child molester who raped her repeatedly while she was in his care. This was better in her mind.

Harriet was still packing when her mother walked in and found her putting the last bit in her bag. She turned out of the room; knowing she was going to get some form of weapon, Harriet, closed the door and braced on it. She began to shake knowing that it wasn't before long that her mother would make her way into the room. Not long after, her mother was kicking in the door. It only took her two kicks to get in. The door swung back on Harriet causing her to fall, hitting her head on the base of the bed. Her mother came in and straddled her, holding a knife point it at her throat.

"Where the fuck do you think you're going gal? You think I'm going to sit here and worry about you or have police coming to my door about your nasty raas? You want to get me in problems? I'll slit your fucking throat if you want to get me in problems! I'll kill you!" she butted her in her forehead with the back of the knife's blade. "You are a fucking disgrace! I wish I had closed my legs and strangled you when you were coming out of me!" She spat on her.

"Kill me then mommy. It's easy. Kill me."

Her mother continued to use the back of the knife to hit her repeatedly in her face. Harriet gave up moving, speaking and crying. She just laid there while her mother beat her with the knife in her face, then shoulders, then her knee and finally the sole of her feet. When her mother left the room, Harriet didn't get up off the ground. She just laid there. She thought of how much more attractive death looked: how she'd be happy on the other side. She opened her palms, pressing them to the wooden floor, then prayed. Her prayer was to be taken from the cruel world she existed in with her mother. She questioned God: how could he really allow these things to happen to her? How could he sit by and watch her mother do these things to her time after time? Didn't he care about her? Did he love her as his child? Why was he allowing her to go through this?

As usual, her mother dressed her wounds while telling her how she had caused her to beat her the way she had later the evening. She told her that she made her angry and that she didn't like having to beat her like that, but she'd left her no choice. She told her she could stay home from school until the swelling on her eye went down and gave her phone to borrow to play Candy Crush. In her mind Harriet told her how wicked she was and how she'd kill her herself if only she had the strength. In her mind, Harriet wished she'd not been born or at least not to her mother. She didn't want to play Candy Crush but she'd play for now and send a message to her friend to ask whether she could stay over for a while, as soon as her mother wasn't looking.

Harriet's friend texted back that she couldn't stay over and she was crushed. She knew she was taking a chance to ask but didn't have anyone else to ask. Her only relative was her aunt who was just as wicked; going there wouldn't do her any good. The last time Harriet had sought refuge in her friend's home her mother had shown up with the police and created a scene. She told the police that Harriet was kidnapped by her friend's mother and it had taken a while to sort it out. It was at the police station that an officer had recognised both Harriet and her mother. He pulled the officer dealing with them aside and told him that Harriet was a regular runaway. The officer knew then that Harriet was telling the truth when she said her friend's mother was only trying to help by allowing her to stay over. Harriet's mother created a scene at the police station because the police refused to charge the lady with kidnapping. They had to threaten her a few times with holding her in the lockup for her to leave.

Harriet was different compared to Susan. She was the type of child who thought that her mother was responsible for her entirely. She was the child who had needs and those needs were to be provided for by her parents. Susan would take whatever she got, whether her needs were met or not. If her mother didn't give her money for transport to school, she would walk the two hours plus journey. If Susan presented the booklist to her mother and she didn't buy the books, she wouldn't remind her or ask for it. She knew her mother understood her needs just as well as she did, hence it wasn't necessary to remind her. Harriet on the other hand would blow a fuse if her needs weren't met. If she woke up and got dressed for school and asked for her lunch and transportation monies and didn't get it, she'd tell her mother she isn't going to school that day. Her mother could afford to send both girls to school with both their fathers providing financial assistance and her having a well-paid job. However, she didn't see the need to always do so. Her own needs and wants were her priority. Instead of buying their textbooks she'd buy brand name shoes and clothes. Before giving them money for school in the morning she'd think about all she needed to do for herself and if her budget couldn't fit them in, there was no way she'd make the sacrifice.

Susan woke up by 4am every morning. In order to get to school by 8am each morning she needed to leave by 5:30am, if she was going to walk. Walking to school also meant that she wouldn't have money for lunch hence, she needed to make sure to prepare and have breakfast and make the usual sandwich to take to school. It was mandatory to clean the living room and kitchen before leaving each morning, so she needed the full 90 minutes to get things done each morning. If her mother gave her money for the bus, she'd still leave at 5:30 sharp and study before school starts. Harriet on the other hand would only take the bus at 7am; walking to school was not an option for her.

She walked into her mother's room and asked for money to go to school. Her mother had been trying to sleep off her hangover and was not happy to be woken up.

"Get out of my room!" she threw the pillow at her and used the second one to cover her head.

"But mommy it's school time so I need money to go. Plus it's getting late now," she hissed her teeth.

"I don't have any money. Leave me alone let me sleep in peace."

"I'm going to take money from your bag because I have a test so I have to go to school today."

"This fucking bitch though!" she screamed, sitting up in her bed. "I'm fucking tired" Get the fuck out and let me sleep!"

"But mommy I need money for school."

"Wait, am I working for you? Where the fuck do you expect me to get money from? Get out of my room now!"

"I have to go to school," Harriet stood there scanning the room for her mother's handbag.

"Why are you telling me that? Go get a man to give you money for school and leave me the fuck alone. I don't have any money to give you and if I have to get up out of this bed to put you out only God can save you."

"I don't want any man's money. Alright, give me the money my father gave your for me to go to school."

"Fuck man!" her mother leaped out of the bed and Harriet ran out of the room.

"Harriet!" She wasn't quick enough to catch her or see where she'd run to. "You want money for school so come for it. Here's the money."

Harriet knew her mother was probably trying to lure her, but she needed to do test. It was her last chance to make up her grades before final exams or she was going to fail maths.

"Harriet!" her mother screamed for her again.

"Yes mommy," she came from under the cellar.

"Where are you? Come for the money."

"I'm outside, throw it out the window and I'll pick it up."

"Come for it or you won't get it."

She was sure now she was being lured, "it's fine. I'm not going to school. It's too late now." She peeped around the side of the house awaiting her mother's response. She was quiet.

Suddenly, Harriet heard her mother behind her and turned around just in time to see the knife coming down. She threw her hand up to block it as the full force of her mother came down with the knife, stabbing her on her forearm.

"Mommy!" Harriet yelled.

Her mother backed away then ran towards her, kicking her in her chest, causing her to collapse to the ground. "I told you to leave me the fuck alone!" She turned and walked away.

Harriet's uniform was covered in blood. She picked herself up from the ground and looked down to see the big open wound oozing blood. She looked around to make sure no one was looking. She felt the fire in her belly, something in her mind telling her to go inside the house and stab her mother right in her heart. She wanted to get equal but knew she was no match for her mother. Then her thoughts shifted to how asking for money for school had come to this. All she was asking of her mother was for her to be responsible and give her money for school. Her mind then made her aware of the fact that she wouldn't make the test and she knew the implications it would have. She walked around to her mother's window to check whether she'd gone back into her room and confirmed that she had.

Harriet didn't have anywhere to go to seek refuge. The only person she could think of going to was her father, but she didn't know where he lived or worked. The only time she'd see him is when he'd stop by their house. She couldn't go to her only aunt she knew or her friend's house. She had no alternative, but she knew she wasn't going to stay in her mother house a moment longer.

She went into her bedroom and tied a cotton shirt around her wound. She then changed into a pair of jeans and a t-shirt, packing another pair of jeans, a few panties, an extra bra and a flat sheet. She gazed at the dresser she shared with her sister and thought of taking some toiletries but decided against it. She laid out her uniform on the bed then wrote "ASK YUH MA!" on it and placed it next to the bloody uniform. She put on a pair of flipflops then went out through the back door and headed into the woods behind their house.

Harriet felt scared going into the unknown, but she didn't care. She wanted to get away from her mother and everything. She'd spent a lot of time alone in the woods and knew that no one frequented it, so no one would be able to find her. Walking into the woods, she continued to gaze at the knot around her arm, constantly trying to make sense of her mother's actions. She soon came upon a big mango tree she's been to before, resting her bag on the ground then sitting on it.

For almost a week no one knew where she was. The police were notified that she was missing, and Susan assumed she was dead. She'd never gone missing this long. Social media sent her photo around with a message that said she was last seen going to school in her uniform but Susan knew this wasn't true. Something had happened that morning that caused her to leave her bloody uniform on the bed. She checked and was sure that none of her sister's uniforms were missing. Susan couldn't focus at school, even her mother didn't seem okay. Susan came home from school on the fourth day her sister had been missing and found their mother in her room crying. She'd never seen this sight before.

"Mommy, what's wrong?"

"What if she bled to death somewhere? What if she's dead? Nobody knows where she is. I've checked everywhere."

"What do you mean bleed to death? How would she bleed to death?

"Susan, I was so upset I stabbed her. I didn't even check to see if she was okay."

"Where did you stab her though?"

"I think on her hand. If she didn't turn around it would have been in her head or her back."

Susan sighed, "but mommy you always do these things without thinking. I'm not trying to be disrespectful but you need to look into yourself and control your temper. You do whatever you want with us, it's like you're trying to kill us. If they find her dead what are you going to tell the police? This needs...."

"Just shut up man!"

"See what I mean. I'm trying to talk to you and you're just getting angry. You need to tell the truth too because everyone is looking for her in her school uniform and she wasn't wearing her school uniform. Someone might have seen her but think it's the wrong person."

"I can't tell them. I already burned the bloody uniform this morning so just keep saying she's in her uniform. It's the face they are looking for anyway."

Susan glared at her mother in disgust. "I was already gone so no one must ask me but if the police ask me, I will tell them the truth."

"Get out of my face because you're making me angry."

Finally, Harriet turned up. She'd been in the woods for six nights and seven days. She was covered in mosquito bites and her wound had a greenish pus of a foul odour coming from it. She'd survived by foraging for fruits in the woods but her hand had developed a numbness she couldn't shake: she wanted to be taken to the doctor.

Their mother met them at the hospital; the police were phoned when they arrived at the hospital and they'd subsequently called her. Harriet wouldn't tell them where she was. Her mother didn't push; she told the police to leave her alone. She didn't want them finding out that she was the one that had stabbed Harriet. Outside the hospital, their mother cried and promised them that she'd never allow her temper to get the better of her again. She apologised to Harriet and begged for her forgiveness.

The promise their mother made to them didn't even last a full day. By the following morning she was throwing things around, annoyed that she had to give the girls money for school. Her behaviour remained the same and she dealt with matters just the same. If she didn't want to, she didn't give them money for school. If she wanted to buy clothes and shoes or go out drinking instead of making sure they were provided for, she would. More importantly, she continued to beat them with whatever she felt like using. Only weeks later, she wrapped a barbed wire around Susan's neck and tried to strangle her with it. Her apology meant nothing.

Close to the end of ninth grade, she was called into school because Harriet had missed too many school days; had failed to pass most of the subjects and was in danger of being held back in her class. The teachers were struggling to move her to a grade ten stream with a subject focus. They were either going to hold her back in grade nine and work with both her and her mother to improve on her options or she was going to be placed into a vocational program.

Arriving at the school, her mother was loud and boisterous. She didn't want to be there, and Harriet didn't want her to be there either. In the meeting, while the teacher was explaining the situation to her, she started quarrelling and picked up the chair to hit Harriet with. The teacher jumped between them and screamed, causing a few teachers and students to come to the classroom to investigate. Two other teachers came into the room and Harriet was sent out of the room. The teachers though that their talk had worked and she had calmed down. No one imagined she would wait for school to dismiss to attack Harriet outside the school gate.

Harriet was walking out of the school's main gate with her friends when she saw her mother running towards her. She ran back into the school yard and her mother chased her.

"Dodge," one student shouted.

Harriet turned around just in time to see the beer bottle heading in her direction. She ran between the two buildings and students started jeering and shouting in chaos. Some laughed to see what was happening. Harriet jumped on the first step to the eight-grade block just in time to miss the bottle aimed at her. She raced up the stairs and went into an empty classroom. She hid under the teacher's desk, hoping her mother hadn't seen where she'd gone. She heard her mother panting outside the classroom then heard her footsteps trail down the block. Harriet came from under the desk and peeked out the classroom's door, looking her mother dead in the eyes. Her mother started running back and Harriet ran out the classroom door and down the stairs, skipping three or four stairs at a time. She ran back into the school yard and her mother stayed upstairs and started throwing bottles at her as soon as she appeared in the yard. The second one hit her in the head breaking when it connected. Harriet didn't stop running. Just as she turned the corner, a bottle hit her dead centre in her back. The pain surged through her. A group of girls she was having differences with saw her coming and one of them stepped right in her path, causing her to fall. She heard the bones in her hand crack when she threw her hand to the ground trying break her fall.

"Awww," Harriet shrieked in pain. She tried to stand up but the sound of students around her laughing crippled her. She felt her mother kicking her and heard the students laughing and knew that there was no way she would be able to show her face in school again. Her mother dragged her to the bus stop as she hung her head in shame, pain throbbing in her wrist, all while the students laughed and jeered.

The following day Harriet's mother travelled with her to school and watched to make sure she entered the school gate. Students pointed at her and laughed as she hung her head and made a B-Line for the girls' bathroom on the seventh-grade block, nearest to the school gate. She hid in the bathroom, watching while her mother got onto the bus. As soon as the bus was out of sight, Harriet came out of the bathroom, through the gate and headed in the opposite direction.

Later in the evening she saw a group of men playing dominoes in the front yard of a broken down old wooden house. She had changed into a bodycon dress and a pair of slippers she had sneaked away in her school bag. She stopped by the fence, gazing over at the game. For a while the men didn't notice her then one of them spotted her and invited her over to join the game. She played with them into the late hours of the evening until she was left alone with the man who resided at the house. He noticed she wasn't leaving and started to make conversation with her. It was almost 10pm and he noticed she had no intentions of going home so he invited her into the house. She spent the night there and as scary as the situation was he didn't try to attack her or made any sexual advances to her. The next morning came and he explained to her that she wasn't welcome to stay because it was not appropriate. He urged her to go home to her mother and she left.

Arriving at the police station, she showed the police her wrist that the gentleman had wrapped up for her with ointment. She told them everything that she was going through and the fact that it was her mother who had stabbed her. She begged them to put her into a children's home but a detective at the station called her mother to take her home.

"Does your mother give you food?" The detective had asked.

"Yes but she doesn't give us money for school and most days I don't even get to go to school because I don't have fare."

"It doesn't matter. You have food at home. She won't always have money to send you to school but it doesn't mean you shouldn't do well. Kids go to school every day without lunch."

"I can't learn on empty stomach. I can't concentrate. And how am I supposed to go to school without fare?"

"Hahahaha," he laughed. "That's the problem with your generation, you don't understand real struggle. Ask your mother if she even had shoes to go to school."

"Then why have children if you can't afford them?"

"No wonder your mother have to beat you. If you were my child I'd kick you in your face right now."

Harriet had to continue at the same school. She started dating an eleventh grader who she thought loved her. Over the summer holidays she found out she was pregnant. Susan was helping her conceal the pregnancy. Neither of them had a plan. They didn't know what to do. There was no telling their mother. She had no way of telling her boyfriend. She didn't have a phone and neither did Susan. She had restrained herself from using her mother's phone to text him in fear that she'd be caught. Her mother would not respond kindly to that.

Susan was helping her sister strap her belly down. The girls locked in their bedroom were laughing uncontrollably after the baby had kicked and frightened Susan as she was busy wrapping her sister with the pair of leggings. A frightened Susan jumped up on her bed pointing at the belly. Harriet burst out laughing and the two girls laughed, unable to articulate any real words.

With the summer progressing, they enjoyed their time together without their mother there. When she was around, Harriet tried her best to stay out of sight sometimes spending entire days in the woods behind their house. Her mother would often get mad looking for her to do something and even once beat Susan almost to death because she wouldn't say where Harriet was.

One early morning before dawn, the girls were in their room sleeping when Harriet was frightened by a shooting sharp pain in her belly. She felt something crash into her stomach and reached out to grab it. Her mother was on the bed above her stepping in her belly. She screamed out, waking Susan up. Susan got up to turn on the light and saw her mother stepping on her sister's belly over and over again. Shock took control of her and she peed herself as she looked down to see the bed soaked in blood. Harriet tried holding on to her mother's foot, but she was moving too fast.

"Help me," she said in a weak voice.

Susan still couldn't move, her knees weakened and she collapsed to the floor.

"I'll kill you before you bring a child into this world," her mother said as she climbed off the bed. "Clean up the room now," she demanded as she left the room.

Ivor

"Debbie, Debbie, Debbie, come quick! Ivor fell off the light post!"

"What do you mean fell off the light post? What is he doing on the light post?"

Debbie jumped down from the doorway of her one-bedroom board house over the single step and went running like mad through the streets to find her son. She was almost naked; wearing only her panty and bra, a bonnet on her head protecting her hairdo. She ran down the street, constantly looking back at the children to reassure herself she was running in the right direction. They struggled to keep up. She was already passing the second street from hers and couldn't see Ivor yet.

"Where is Ivor, where is Ivor?" she asked frantically.

No one responded though, the kids kept running, trying to keep up with her; pointing ahead each time. When she finally saw Ivor up ahead, she sprang further into action running faster to him. Reaching him, she grabbed him up from the ground, his limp body not responding.

"What happened to him? What happened to my pickney?" she screamed at everyone around her, but no one respond. Realising that no one was going to help her, she began to run back towards her house with him cradled in her arms. Eight years old Ivor felt like a baby in her hand, her motherly instincts had kicked in and her strength was unrecognisable. While running, Ivor moved in her hand and for the first time she realised that he was completely wet, soaked from head to toe. Relief fell over her and she fell to her knees wrapping him tighter in her arms and breaking into tears.

"Mommy, you're squeezing me too tight." He coughed a forceful cough as if to get his point across.

"Hush baby. Ivor what happened?"

"Nothing mommy."

"Don't tell me nothing happened, how did you fall off the light post? What were you doing up there?"

"Mommy, nothing happened. Let's go home. You need to put on clothes."

"Tell me the truth and stop telling me foolishness. What happened? Don't let me have to ask again."

"Mommy, I promise I'm going to tell you. But can we please go home, and you put clothes on please? I will tell you at the house."

Debbie knew how easily embarrassed Ivor got and she was very protective of him, so she decided to get off the street in her underwear. Walking back, she wouldn't let go off him. The shy young boy wouldn't lift his eyes off the ground. He was mortified. As many times as his mother had come out in the street often wearing nothing but a pair of panties, he was still embarrassed every single time.

"Debbie you again? What happened now?" Tasha down the road enquired as Ivor and Debbie were passing her gate.

"Don't start. As a matter of fact, I won't even answer you. Let me walk in peace." She hissed her teeth and continued walking home with Ivor under her arm. "Think she's seen anything yet, wait until I put on my clothes and come back out." She mumbled.

"Mommy, stop please." Ivor begged.

"Alright, alright, come."

It was a regular thing for Ivor to be taken advantage of in his community. Debbie was a single mother with no father figure for Ivor or family close by, she worked long hours as a security guard which meant Ivor was often at home by himself and everyone in the community took advantage of that. Any and everyone would send Ivor to the shop night or day once Debbie wasn't around. He'd often be called by a neighbour to sweep their yard or help with other chores. Hilda who lived across the road from them, made it a regular habit for him to wash her pots after dinner whenever his mother wasn't around. The boys in the neighbourhood often ganged up on him and even grown men and women regularly assaulted him.

Complaining to his mother often lead to a huge brawl between her and whoever had illtreated him. In one incident, his mother was stabbed by Biggs who had kicked

Ivor in his back while on his way from the shop. Debbie had heard Chris bawling, had looked outside to see his face muddy, a boot print on the back of his t-shirt and him holding his back. When she enquired, one of the kids in the street had said that Biggs kicked him and Debbie flew into rage and attacked Biggs. She was no match for the 6ft plus man, but she fought. Debbie punched and kicked and threatened to burn him with acid. When she ripped his shirt off and bit his arm wrapped around her neck, he stabbed her with his pocket knife. It was only then that the men looking on, decided to break up the fight.

Ivor never forgot this incident, or the time Hilda and her sister Betty had ganged his mother when his mother attacked Hilda for beating Ivor while she was at work. Those two incidents made him realise that he only had his mother and he was better off being treated badly by the people in his community than losing his mother. She had no one to help her fight them. He was too young, too small. He couldn't even defend himself against other kids, let alone the adults. Ivor made up his mind that he would try very hard to cover up what he was going through. He started to lie to her. Often.

Ivor was a result of an affair Debbie had with a married man, who broke it off with her the moment he found out she was pregnant. Debbie thought long and hard about having an abortion at the request of her mother but decided that she wanted to have the baby. This decision shaped her life and in turn his. Her mother was a deaconess at the church she grew up in and couldn't stand the shame of her teenage daughter having a child; so, she shunned Debbie and wanted nothing to do with her grandchild. Her father died years earlier and her grandparents and aunt refused to take her in. Her uncle who was living abroad had taken pity on her and sent her some money. Knowing that difficult times were ahead, and she couldn't fully rely on anyone, she had used most of the money to pay for a bedroom inside a tenement yard and kept enough to pay her rent for a few months. She immediately got a job working in a clothing wholesale as a cashier.

For most of his life it was just the two of them. His mother was never out of work. When she left a job, she started another one by the following week. Everything she had, everything she did was for the two of them and Ivor knew this. She made sure there was enough food in the house, Ivor had money for school every day, he had clean clothes and all his needs were taken care of. She couldn't afford much though. The one-bedroom board house was an upgrade from their previous home. His mother always told him that one day they would buy their own home but until then they would have to make do with what they could afford.

Debbie worked long hours: most days she did a double shift. She'd only get home late at nights and would be up to get Ivor and herself ready early in the mornings. She made sure his dinner was prepared every single day. There was a TV in the room for him to watch when he got home, do his homework, bathe then go to bed after locking up properly. She'd call him often to make sure he was okay. She imagined that when she couldn't get him, it was because he was playing which she didn't approve of but knew he was lonely left all on his own almost every day. She wanted to spend more time with him but had to take as many shifts as she could so that she could save and take care of them. She had no one else to depend on for help. By then her uncle living abroad had retired and though he'd call to check they were okay every now and then, he never provided any financial help. If she didn't have, they didn't have.

Peter was one of those guys always on the street corner as though he was assigned neighbourhood watch. As far as Debbie knew, he'd never had a job; she didn't know whether he'd had an education either. Initially she resented him. She thought him a mere waste of space, lazy and too comfortable with where he was at. But as time went by, he'd help her out and she had grown fond of him. On her days off she'd cook and call him to come over for food. He made advances at her, but she didn't give in. She wasn't interested in him romantically. Her focus was on working hard to create a better life for her and her son and someone like Peter couldn't provide any form of security or had the qualities she was looking for in a partner.

One day Ivor was ill with the flu and she was scheduled for a double, which meant leaving him all alone early in the morning and returning late at night. Peter volunteered to stay with him, but she didn't take up the offer as she'd only worry whether Ivor was okay and wouldn't be able to focus at all. This offer made by Peter however, presented an opportunity in itself. She was always worried whether Ivor was okay when she worked late, and she didn't exactly have anyone she could rely on to help her with him. She thought she could depend on Hilda but that didn't turn out well, so Ivor was left to look after himself and he was young. She made a deal with Peter, he would check on Ivor in the evenings and make sure he'd eaten and in bed at a reasonable time and in return Debbie would give him a bit of cash on the weekends.

The first night when Peter turned up to check on Ivor he was already in bed. It was already after 9pm and Ivor was fast asleep. He couldn't hear him knocking outside.

"What did you and Peter do last night?" Debbie questioned the following morning.

"Peter? Peter that you give food?"

"Who else Ivor? Didn't he come yesterday?"

"No mommy, I saw him on the road when I was coming from school, but he didn't come over here."

"Oh, he was supposed to come. I'll call him and see what happened later."

"Mommy I can look after myself. Don't let him come."

"I know baby, but it's good for someone to be near in case anything happens."

"Nothing will happen."

"Well you never know. He'll just come in the evenings and stay until I get back from work."

"Mommy you worry too much, I'm alright by myself."

"I have to worry. Come, let's get ready."

In the afternoon Debbie called Peter who apologised for not showing up, who said he'd forgotten but promised he'd go by in the evening. He kept his promise and went by early evening. Ivor had already had dinner and was watching TV. It was the first of many sittings and went smoothly.

It started off as subtle incidents made to seem like accidents. Peter would pretend to drop a glass or a plate or anything heavy on Ivor's head accidently. He'd stand above him sitting on the hassock and drop a glass full of water on his head then say sorry, pretending as though it had fallen by accident. On one occasion he pretended he'd not realised Ivor was still holding on the door and slammed it shut, crushing his fingers. Something inside told Ivor that they weren't accidents, so he never told his mother about any of the incidents. When Debbie saw his four fingers on his right hand swollen, he told her that he'd closed the door on them himself.

Peter started showing up at the house earlier and he got more brazen with how he was treating Ivor. There was always enough food left for the two of them to eat twice if they needed to, Debbie made sure of it, and it had always served them well. Peter started a new trend. As soon as Ivor would open the door, he would find his way to the pots and would eat every bit of food in them. Ivor would often end up having to go to bed without food. Eventually he started hiding away snacks to make sure he had something to eat after school. He'd save some of his lunch or pack snacks in his bag before school and eat them on his way home.

Peter also started controlling what he did in the evenings. It was routine for Ivor to watch TV after school before and after doing his homework. It was a deal he had with his mother: as long as he did his homework, he could watch as much TV as he wanted to. She preferred him in the house where she was sure he was safe, so the TV was his company. She never bothered him with it. Whatever he watched was what she watched.

His TV privileges were soon revoked by Peter. In the evenings Peter would sit him in a corner facing the wall while he controlled the remote. If Ivor laughed at something he heard while eavesdropping, Peter would get up from the bed and slap him in the back of his head, pull his ears or even kick him in his lower back and tell him not to listen. He soon took it up a notch by stuffing Ivor's ears with toilet paper, tying his hands behind him and blindfolding him each time before seating him in the corner of the room next to the fridge. When it first started Ivor would cry and cry and beg him to stop: but soon he realised that it wasn't worth the kick, punch or slap he would get.

One evening Ivor came home from school to find that Peter wasn't waiting on him outside his house. He locked the door behind him and hurried to the pots of food his mother left the same morning for his and Peter's dinner. Still in his uniform, Ivor got the pots of the stove and onto the floor. Armed with his fingers, he dug into the rice and kidneys. He ate and ate until he was stuffed and physically couldn't eat even an additional grain of rice. Overwhelmed with pleasure that he'd beaten Peter to it, Ivor laid back on the floor with a grand smile on his face. It dawned on him that Peter would be angry and beat him, but he pushed the idea to the back of his mind. For the moment he wanted to enjoy the fact that he was full. He'd come home from school and had his dinner.

When he could finally move, Ivor got up from the floor and took up the pots with the rest of the food. There wasn't much left. He toyed with the idea of hiding the rest of the food and washing the pots. For a slight moment, he wanted Peter to feel what he'd felt all those evenings. Then the thought of Peter beating him resurfaced again. Soon he heard Peter talking outside and fear filled him. He quietly replaced the second pot cover, put his bag back on his back and opened the back door. He peeped outside to see that no one was there and climbed down the back step, quietly closing the door behind him. Ivor peeped around the side of the house and when he couldn't see Peter he ran behind the neighbour's house. He walked quietly behind a few of the houses then finally between two houses, almost touching each other, and came back on the main road.

"Wait, Ivor, didn't you just pass me down the road?"

"No Miss Karen, I'm just coming from school," he fastened his pace.

"Hm, I could have sworn he just passed by," she said to herself puzzlingly.

Peter questioned Ivor about the amount of food in the pots that evening. He lied, telling him that his mother did not have enough to cook in the morning. Peter believed him. As usual, he ate all the food in the pots and gave none to Ivor. Usually Ivor would cry and even beg but today he was full.

"Mommy, can I come to your work after school please?"

"Not today baby, I'm doing a double and I can't keep you out that late, you have school tomorrow."

"Please mommy, I can sleep in the office with Mr Stephens until you finish working. Please, can I come mommy?"

"Ivor, I told you already, no. Not tonight."

He began to cry. "Mommy, please can I just come after school?"

"Ivor come here," she sat of the foot of her bed. "What's wrong? Why are you crying? Did something happen?"

"Mommy I don't want to stay with Peter."

"Wait, did he do something to you?"

"No mommy."

"Ivor tell me the truth. You know you can tell mommy anything."

"I just don't want to stay with him." Ivor continued to cry.

"You mustn't lie to me. Something happened. Tell me what happened." Debbie could feel herself getting angry, but she contained it. She knew something was wrong. What was it? What was she missing?

"I'll stay with him, nothing happened."

"No, no, no. Come to work after school. I'll pack something for you, so you can change your uniform."

After school Ivor met his mother at her workplace. For the first time in a long time he found some peace after school. He sat in the guards-room, doing his homework then later had the Double-Whopper his mother bought him. She initially thought of bringing his dinner to work but decided to get him a treat. She knew something was wrong though he wasn't telling her.

Peter called the entire evening, but Debbie ignored his call. She was too angry to talk to him even though she didn't know what he'd done to Ivor. She planned to invite him over on her day off to 'have a talk'.

The following day Debbie had Ivor come to her at work again. She was working the weekend and took him to work with her. Her boss complained about it on the second day but Debbie pleaded with him to allow her just until she could sort out an alternative. Her boss gave the okay.

Monday came and it was Debbie's day off so she sent Peter a message inviting him over for dinner. Although he hadn't heard from her for a few days, he took up the offer and met her at her house early afternoon.

"I said to come for dinner," Debbie said with sarcasm, "it's barely past lunch time."

"Hahaha, no man. I came early to see if you needed help with anything."

"Okay sir. Being that you're here, let's cut right to the chase." Debbie felt the anger growing inside her but knew she needed to keep calm to see if she'd get any truth from him.

"Which chase now?"

"No man wait, it's coming. So, you remember the other day when Ivor came home from school beaten up, did he tell you what happened?"

"Yes of course I remember. You need to go down to that school and sort it out because they're always beating him up at school."

"Did he tell you about what happened?"

"No, not at all. I asked him, but he didn't tell me a thing."

"Really, I thought he would, being that you saw him before me. Okay."

Debbie had gone down to the school on Friday. She spoke with the teacher again about several incidents Ivor had claimed occurred at school. She wanted to be sure. When Ivor had complained to her; about being beaten up at school, getting a blackeye at school, getting the bruises on his back at school, getting the beer bottle shaped scars on his knees at school and having chest pains from getting into a fight at school, she'd gone to his teacher to investigate each incident. The teacher wasn't aware of any of them and each time promised she'd look into it but each time she'd come back saying Ivor wouldn't tell her which boys he'd fought with and none of the kids knew about it. Debbie went back on Friday though to see whether the teacher had found out anything since their last talk. The more she thought about it, the more obvious it was that the person responsible for doing all those things to Ivor could only be Peter. This was the reason Ivor didn't want to be around him.

Debbie was angry with herself for not noticing sooner that something was wrong. No matter how much she asked Ivor whether Peter had hurt him, Ivor wouldn't tell her the truth.

"Peter, Ivor told you about his chest pains?"

"He mentioned something about that the other day, but he didn't really tell me much."

"Really, what else did he tell you about?"

"You know, just little things here and there but the boy doesn't really talk much."

"Yes, he's quiet. Anyway, enough talking. Help me move this pan."

Debbie realised that Peter wasn't going to tell her the truth or cop to anything, so she moved to Plan B. Ivor didn't know that she was going to be home. In the morning she told Ivor that she was taking an afternoon shift so would be gone by the time she got home. She explained to him that he couldn't come to work and told him that she'd tell Peter not to come by so the boy would be alone. Peter didn't know that Ivor wasn't expecting him.

When it got close to the time for Ivor to come home, Debbie asked Peter to wait outside while she ran a quick errand in town. She asked him to wait for Ivor and explained that Ivor had his key and would let him in. Her excuse for not leaving him in the house was that Ivor wasn't expecting anyone to be there and she didn't want him to be frightened if he came home to find him in the house. Peter believed her. He waited outside, watched Debbie go into a bus up the road then planted himself on an empty five-gallon paint bucket outside Debbie's door.

Ivor was not pleased to see Peter waiting outside his house. He stood across the road and called his mother on the phone, but she didn't answer. Neither of the two knew that Debbie was outside her backdoor waiting to see what would unfold between the two of them. Debbie sent Ivor a text message telling him to go inside and she'd call him back as soon as she could. The boy sat on the sidewalk across the road, his head hanging between his legs not wanting to go into his house to deal with the man who'd been tormenting him nonstop. He messaged his mother back to tell her that Peter was outside their house and that he didn't need a baby sitter. His mother messaged him back telling him to go into the house immediately and that she'd call Peter as soon as she got the chance.

Peter didn't notice that Ivor had come home from school and was across the street because his face was covered with his hat while he leaned against the house to take a nap.

"Good evening," Ivor said waking Peter.

"Little man, you're home now."

"My name is Ivor, not little man."

"Hold on, who do you think you're talking to? Fix up your face too before I," he raised his had to hit Ivor and Ivor ducked.

"Don't know why you don't leave and go to your yard," Ivor mumbled under his breath.

"What did you say? Speak up so I can hear you."

Debbie was boiling but wanted to wait for it all to unfold before she'd get involved. She wanted to know exactly what Peter was doing to her son.

"I said you must go to your yard. My mother said you can't come back here. Everyday you come and torment me. Go to your hard."

"Boy, who do you think you're talking to? I'll kick you across your face and let all your teeth fly!"

Ivor bowed his head in defeat. His mother hadn't called back so there was no way of stopping Peter from coming into the house. He imagined it would be another evening of Peter pushing him around, hitting or kicking him and he wasn't up for it. He'd grown tired of tiptoeing around his own house trying to stay out of Peter's way and being hit for no reason other than the fact that Peter wanted to hit hm.

"By the way, what did you tell your mother? She keeps asking a lot of questions, so I know you told her something."

"I didn't tell mommy anything about you."

"You better make sure because remember, I will slit her throat in front of you," he pushed Ivor's forehead.

"I didn't say anything," Ivor shrugged.

Hearing this was enough for Debbie. She got up from the step with the bleach in one hand and the piece of steel she'd prepared for this very moment. She knocked on the back door and Ivor moved to open it, but Peter pushed him out of the way to do it himself. Although he was expecting Debbie back, he expected her to come through the front door. He suspected it was the regular; a neighbour begging this or that. He opened the back door and Debbie doused his eyes with the bleach. He staggered, covering his head with both hands screaming. His screams got louder when Debbie began to beat him with the steel. He fell to the ground and she kept beating him. Ivor had jumped onto the bed and had retreated to the far corner. He was shaking.

Neighbours heard Peter's screams and called the police.

Police took Debbie away that night and Hilda took the task of watching over Ivor. For days, all Ivor did was cry for his mother. No one was taking him to see her and he didn't know whether she was okay. He struggled to eat or sleep. Hilda showed him no sympathy; he was just another set of hands in her house. When he asked about his mother, she'd shout at him to leave her alone; she provided no information or showed any concerns for how he was coping.

At school, Ivor told his teacher what had happened and what was happening. His mother was taken by the police, he didn't know where she was and instead of helping him find her, Hilda was working him to the ground and treating him poorly. His teacher brought him to see the principal, where he had to repeat what he'd told her. Calling the police station, his principal found out that Peter had succumbed to his injuries at the hospital and Debbie was being charged with murder. His next phone call was to arrange collection of Ivor by the state.

Ivor was brought to collect his things at home by a woman in a minivan after school. He didn't know her. They packed his bags into the van and drove away. They arrived at a home with 17 other boys. The lady who travelled with him in the minivan, introduced and handed him over to another lady who took him to a room and showed him a bed. It was the bottom bunk in a row of bunk beds next to the wall. Ivor sat on the bed as she left the room. Other boys came in and tried to make conversation, but inside Ivor felt sad, alone and afraid without his mother.

The first few nights he didn't sleep, he laid awake thinking about his mother and how she was. No one was telling him anything directly. He didn't know whether she was alive or dead. He knew nothing.

Life in the boy's home was okay at first but it soon became a nightmare and his mother wasn't there to protect him.

Today, as a man, Ivor has many scars on his body and face from the abuse he faced as a child; both before the boy's home and during. His mother is doing a life sentence for the murder of the man who abused him as a boy and he is still as close to her as he were, before she went away.

Lakresha

Lakresha's earliest memory is of her two years old self being held face down in a bucket of water; her tiny little legs kicking, her screaming and taking water in. She's sure she was only two because the first time she mentioned it to her eldest sister, she was shocked that she'd remember as she was merely two years old, nowhere near three. Lakresha remembers herself screaming and her little body collapsing to the ground, thankful for the air around her. Her lungs, barely developed, ached terribly. Her sister told her of the full story when she recalled the memory and asked her about it.

Their mother was angry because she had defecated on herself and used her mess to create a not so pleasant piece of art on the kitchen door leading to the back yard. When she was summoned by the next-door neighbour to attend to Lakresha, she had flown into a rage. She picked her up by the back of her neck and dumped her in a basin of water perched on the outside wash stand. She continued to beat her while bathing her, all the while Lakresha was screaming.

"I'm tired of you! I'm fucking tired of you!" She got angrier; she spanked her harder then held Lakresha's head down in the water. Lakresha was fighting and kicking her tiny legs with all her might. She kicked her mother and in reaction she pulled her from under the water and thumped her three times in her back then dumped her again face down into the water. Her older brother Lenny came rushing into the yard, holding onto his mother's leg hitting her and begging her to stop. Their older sister watched from the backroom's window but couldn't do anything to help. She couldn't even call for help. She was her mother's punching bag only the day before and was badly hurt. Sonya came home late from school and was beaten with everything in her mother's reach. Her mother strangled her with some electrical wire. She woke up with no voice, a swollen face and bloody sheets from her wounds. Sheets she had hiding under her bed because she didn't want another dose of beating for having messed up the sheets.

Lenny kept pulling his mother but she wouldn't release the baby so he grabbed her thigh and sunk his teeth into it. She kicked him off her and he went crashing into the drum filled with water near the fence. She pulled Lakresha out of the water and dropped her on the ground next to the sink. Lenny tried to get up, but he wasn't quick enough. His mother walked over to him and kicked him repeatedly, until her right leg was tired. She continued with her left leg but that didn't last long. When she was done, she dragged him by his right foot over to where Lakresha was lying; his back dragging on the gravelled ground. Lakresha cried while her sister recalled the story and begged her to stop without finishing. She couldn't hear anymore.

"Twinkle twinkle little star," tears trailed down Sonya's cheeks and she tried to soothe her sister's pain with butter and her favourite song, "how I wonder what you are. Up above the world so high," she went quiet.

"Sing Yaya, sing." Lakresha's feint voice beckoned. She was numb from the pain.

"Then you show your little light…"

"No Yaya, not right. Diamond in the sky."

Sonya giggled at the thought that her sister had so much fight. Both hands were badly burnt.

Earlier that day Sonya was tasked to make dinner. She forgot to add salt to the pot and her mother was annoyed with her. She said her mind was set on the pumpkin soup and Sonya had ruined it for her. Lakresha was sat on the floor eating her dinner. Their mother got up in anger with her soup in hand and tripped over Lakresha, the soup spilled and burned her on her hand. Sonya rushed to the scene to clean up the mess and move Lakresha out of the way. Her mother grabbed Lakresha out of her hand and walked into the kitchen with her, dumping both her hands into the pot of soup on the stove. The four years old girl gave out a bellowing scream and began to cry uncontrollably. Sonya grabbed her and rushed to the fridge to grab the butter. Her mother threatened to hit her, but she didn't care, she needed to save her baby sister.

No doctor saw to the burns and Lakresha haven't outgrown the scars either. Whenever someone asks her about the scars, she'd always tell them she had an accident when she was young but never ever went into what had happened.

By the time Lakresha got to the age of seven, her mother had retired from all her house duties. It was the responsibility of the children to clean, wash, cook, iron and keep the yard clean. If things weren't done on time or to her standards, there were consequences which none of them could easily bear. Sonya was once stabbed with a fork for not seaming her mother's blouse correctly and Lenny has a broken tooth for not sweeping up the yard on time. Between them the children have over 100 scars on their bodies they can associate with their mother. They were battered for anything and everything. None of them can remember a time they were forgiven for a mistake or showed any form of sympathy by their mother. Lakresha remembers her brother coming home badly beaten up by a gang of boys from school and instead of doing something about it, their mother beat him and poured salt into the scar on his face which he'd gotten in the fight.

On her ninth birthday, Sonya told Lakresha that she didn't have to lift a finger as she'd be at her service for a full 24 hours. She would take over all her chores and would cook her favourite meal, curried chicken with dumplings for her that day. Their mother had unplugged the phone line and taken the cord with her to work so there was no way for her to call to put a dinner request in. Sonya would make dinner with only Lakresha in mind. It was going to be a good birthday for her, their mother would only be coming home late evening. It was supposed to be a happy day.

Before heading out to work their mother gave Lakresha the task of polishing her church shoes for the following day but Lakresha forgot. She didn't tell Sonya that this task was added to her day's roster, so it wasn't done. To the children's surprise, their mother came home from work early. She got home at around 3pm to find Lakresha's hair combed and beaded, wearing her favourite green lambada dress.

"Whose beads are in her hair?"

"It's hers, I bought them at school for her?"

"With which money?"

"I saved up my lunch money and bought them."

"Okay, so you're getting too much money to go to school then. You can afford to waste my fucking money on beads!" she started raising her voice.

"No, but it's her birthday. I wanted to do something nice for her."

"Gal, are you giving me chat in my own house? You want to lose all you fucking teeth? Pull them out and bring back the beads and get back my fucking money. As a matter of fact, eat the beads for lunch for the rest of the term."

"Let her keep the beads in her hair. You don't have to give me any lunch money." Evidence of both defiance and annoyance trailed in her voice.

"Who the hell do you think you're talking to gal?"

"Nobody."

She started slapping Sonya in her face, "you're too fucking bright for your own fucking good. I won't live in here with no woman, so keep talking and see if you don't end up on the street with not even the clothes on your back."

Sonya took the slaps and didn't cry. "Alright," she shrugged.

"Lenny, bring the scissors let me cut out these damn beads."

"I'll loose it out, you don't need to cut her hair."

"Oh so now you're telling me what to do in my house too. Lenny bring me the scissors now!"

"I'm not telling you what to do."

Lenny didn't move. "Lenny! Scissors! NOW!"

"Mommy, Yaya will take them out," a scared Lakresha contributed.

"You, move! Sit over there until I'm ready for you!"

Lakresha started sobbing.

"Lenny, what's taking you so long? Don't let me have to come in there to find the scissors myself otherwise you will get it too."

"I don't see them." Lenny lied. He found the scissors and quietly opened the window to drop them outside.

"Oh, so the three of you want to gang up on me. Fine! Where's the big knife?" She shuffled around in the kitchen to find the knife. She picked up the knife and walked over to Lakresha and began cutting her hair with it. Beads locked around the child's hair fell to the ground. Lakresha cried while her older sister looked on, filled with fury. Her brother hiding away in his mother's room.

Sonya tried to comfort her sister, her hair had been made a mess of by their mother and her cornrows unravelled. She didn't bother to recomb it out of fear that it would further anger her mother and make a bad birthday worse. Unbeknown to the three children, Lakresha's birthday was about to get worse, whether they wanted it to or not; much worse.

Lenny and Sonya were outside trying everything they could to make their sister laugh. It didn't seem to be working, she kept touching her hair and her eyes remained sad. Soon a shoe came whizzing pass them, the second foot grazed the top of Sonya's head as she looked around to see what was going on.

"Come here Lakresha!" she yelled.

Sonya hid her sister behind her. Her mother started towards them and Lenny took off running. Lakresha held on to Sonya, locking her hands around her. Her mother pulled and tried to pry her hands apart, but she held on.

"Yaya don't let her take me," she cried.

"Let go! I can't get any fucking peace in this house because of you. Before I go to work you stress me out and I must come home to more stress from you! Sonya, let her go." She punched Sonya in her stomach, but she didn't budge.

"I'll clean them now mommy. I forgot. Sorry mommy."

"Sorry? Bet you'll never forget again after today. This fucking bitch," she was frustrated, "let go before I use something to chop you!"

"Just, leave her. What did she do? If you want the shoes cleaned, I'll clean them. Just leave her alone. It's her birthday, can't you give us a break even for one day?"

She folded her fist and punched Sonya so hard she fell backwards on top of Lakresha. "Don't fuck yourself with me gal!"

She pulled Lakresha from under Sonya. Sonya held on to Lakresha's legs, trying to pull her away from her mother but she wasn't successful. Their mother dragged her to the back of the yard and tied her to the tree. It was her special tree for punishment. It was home to fire ants that nested in its bark. No sooner would she tie one of the kids to the tree than their bodies would be covered by ants, biting into their flesh. She stood and watched Lakresha beg for her to help her and did nothing. The whole time Sonya was trying to figure out how to stop her once and for all.

Sonya rushed to the front yard over the fence and into her neighbour's house.

"Ms Pam, can you come help her please." She was crying now.

"Sonya, you know I can't do anything. Your mother just wants you all to be good children. She's doing the best she can. A little flogging won't harm any of you in the long run."

"Ms Pam, it's harming us now let alone in the long run. She tied Lakresha to the fire-ants tree. Just do something please."

"Aw boy. We all have to go through this Sonya. I went through it, your mother went through it, now you're going through it and so will your children. You just have to raise good children and parents have to be strong to make sure you turn out good. Lakresha will be fine. It's just a bit of discipline."

"Discipline? Ms Pam, I swear if you don't help I'll take a knife and stab her. I swear I will."

"Hey, don't you dare say a thing like that. That is your mother you are talking about. No one will ever love you like your mother. What is a little strapping and punishment? You relax yourself and let your mother do what she'd doing. The more you fight with her, the angrier you will make her and make things worse."

"Ms Pam, please I'm begging you, just tell her to stop please. I'm begging you, please."

"Mighty Jesus our Lord, come let me see what I can do."

"Thanks Ms Pam."

"Oh don't thank me yet, let's hope I don't make things worse. Come on then."

Ms Pam was right, their mother never listened to her pleading to untie Lakresha from the tree. In the end she had given up and decided to go back to her own house and leave their mother to carry out her own means of 'discipline'. By the time she had given Sonya permission to untie Lakresha, her entire body was covered in bites. She could barely walk but she had to clean her mother's shoes still. No amount of pleading with their mother helped.

Sonya searched the entire house for the talcum powder to soothe the itch on her sister's skin but she couldn't find it anywhere. She was sure that her mother had hidden it. She sneaked Lenny out of the house to get aloe vera from the back yard and back in with it.

The kids spent the night plotting to run away, but they had nowhere to go. Their first and only attempt to their father had resulted in him keeping them for a night then returning them to their mother early the next morning and they paid the price. For an entire week their mother gave them nothing to eat; no food whatsoever and they still had to carry out their chores. It affected Lenny the most, so as soon as Lakresha mentioned running away he reminded her of how things had turned out the time they tried that. They agreed it would be best waiting until they were older so they could get a house for the three of them and have nothing to do with their mother.

One day Lakresha's mother saw her coming from school, walking alongside one of the neighbourhood boys. The kids were never allowed outside the yard except for school and church. They were all ashamed of anyone finding out about what they endured at home so they pretty much kept to themselves at school. However, a few of the kids in the neighbourhood took pity on them and would try to chat them up whether on their own or together when they saw them outside of the yard. Their best opportunity would be when they were coming from school.

Lakresha met him on the way home walking from the taxi. He lived quite a few houses before hers but he wanted to walk her home. He'd done this on quite a few occasions. Most times, they did not exchange a word more than 'hi' along the way. He dropped her at the gate and turned to walk back home. Their mother watched the two kids coming up the street engaged in conversations with each other. The boy was telling Lakresha about his little sister who had scared their mom and how his mom was so frightened she fell face first in the dog's poo. The story made Lakresha laugh and she felt warm inside when he told her that their mother had laughed so hard and peed herself. Lakresha was surprised that she didn't beat them.

Her mother waited with belt in her hand for Lakresha to enter the house. Neither of the other kids were home yet.

"Why is he walking you to the gate?"

"Good afternoon mommy."

"Don't good afternoon me! Why is he coming to your gate?"

"He just wanted to walk with me mommy."

"Oh, so this is what happens while I'm at work slaving away for you? You're ready for man?"

"What do you mean mommy? He's just my friend."

"Friend hmm, friend until you're pregnant. Do you think you're bringing any baby in here?"

"Mommy...."

"Don't 'mommy' me. You fucking little bitch! You're only 11 and ready to whore around, you little slut." She started beating Lakresha.

She paused the beating and ordered Lakresha to take her school uniform off. When Lakresha didn't take it off quick enough, she ripped the blouse off and continued to beat her, telling her after each belting to shut up, not to cry. Her clothes became soaked with perspiration and her arms grew tired, so she finally stopped the beating.

For the next few weeks Lakresha's mother only gave her enough money for bus fare to and from school. The punishment was ongoing and that meant not having lunch at school. She wanted to teach Lakresha what it would be like to have to take care of a child all on her own. The young child was puzzled as to why her mother was doing this to her but she wasn't surprised or questioned the beating or the punishment too much. It was her mother and she gave out cruel punishments for the simplest of things.

Before her twelfth birthday, Lakresha's sister Sonya was kicked out of the house. She turned eighteen and according to her mother it was time to 'go make it on her own'. Poor Sonya had nowhere to go. Her mother didn't even have the courtesy of allowing her to take her clothes. While cleaning the house, she asked Sonya to stop to make her a cup of tea in between. Sonya asked her to give her a minute to do is as she was busy washing the toilet and her hands were covered in bleach. Their mother walked into the bathroom and dragged Sonya out by her hair to make the tea. Sonya made the tea and handed it to her mother who threw the tea back at her. The soup smelled of bleach she complained.

"You know what," she looked up at Sonya, "leave. Get out of my house."

Sonya turned to walk out the back door but she stopped her. "No don't go into my yard either. I meant to leave, leave and don't come back."

"What do you mean don't come back? Where must I go?"

"Do I look like I care? Take your ass out and don't come back."

Sonya was wearing a ripped dress she wore on Saturdays to do her cleaning. It had bleach stains all over it and was almost see through. It was an old dress she'd been wearing for years. The fabric was worn. She motioned towards their room to get her clothes.

"What, am I not speaking loud enough? I said to leave now. Don't go anywhere else except through the front door!"

"I need my uniform to go to school."

"Hahahahahaahahaha, but look at this father God," she laughed. "There's no need getting the uniforms, didn't you say the only thing left to do at school are the exams?"

"Yes, my first exam is next Thursday."

"Leave the uniform and everything else. You won't pass the exams anyway so no point going."

"I have to go do my exams," Sonya turned towards the room again.

"Gal, I said to come out of my fucking house," she jumped up and grabbed Sonya by her hair. She dragged her out the front door and into the street. She kept kicking her until two male neighbours pulled her away.

Ms Pam allowed Sonya to stay with them for the day and called her father to come get her but he wouldn't come by until the following day. Lakresha and Lenny cried the whole day and night. Lakresha couldn't sleep. In the night while her mother slept, she took out a uniform skirt and blouse for Sonya and hid it amongst her own clothes. She didn't know how but she would get the uniform to Sonya somehow. The kids had their plan and they didn't want their mother ruining it.

Their mother had previously burnt Sonya's books as punishment. Consequently, she'd made it a habit to always hide her books away, so her mother wouldn't get hold of them. Her only friend at school kept most of them for her on any given day but to study and do homework she had the ones she needed in the house, hidden under the floorboard under their bed. This was where the kids hid all their valuables; money they were saving up, gifts they'd bought each other, pretty much anything they didn't want their mother to know about or get hold of. Lakresha planned to take the books out the first chance she got so that her sister could study for her exams. Her passing meant everything to them.

The following day, Lakresha and Lenny came home from church with their mother to find their father waiting with

Sonya outside the house. Lakresha ran to her father hugging him tight. She turned and hugged her sister then immediately started crying.

"Don't cry, she'll beat you." Sonya dried her sister's eyes.

"What's wrong with you? Why are you taking out your problems on the children?"

"Look here, allow me to come into the yard that I pay rent for in peace. If you have a problem with the job I'm doing, take them with you, it's that simple."

"Yeah man because you know they have to depend on you that's why you treat them like that. Where am I going to put them?"

"Exactly my point. You don't have a place to put them so you don't have a say in what I do or don't do with them."

"This is why I can't deal with you. You just always talk a load of shit and act like some mad woman. I can't rent a bigger place and still pay for this place and you refuse to give me all three of them so I would still have to send you money every week, how must I manage all of that?"

"Give you all of them, you can't even take care of yourself let alone take are of them. And I keep telling you, you don't need to send your money here."

"Yeah and if I'm late one day you have police hunting for me with summons. You take me for a fool."

She opened the door and their father entered taking Sonya with him. "Listen to me and listen to me good, she needs to get out of my house. I'm the only woman in here. Two bull can't reign in one pen and Sonya won't beat me off in here. So, the two of you kindly step outside and we'll talk there. I need to change my church clothes."

Their father hissed his teeth, "you must be sick in your head. I help to pay the rent so that my children have a place to live so don't tell her to stand outside as if she's garbage. As a matter of fact, give me her things so we can leave."

"She has nothing in here, the two of you can leave now."

"Daddy I need my uniforms, they're in our room."

"Then go and take them and come, because I can't deal with your mother and her madness."

"Let her set foot in there and you see which God she's serving today!" their mother yelled from her room.

"Yow, stop the madness. Sonya, get your things and come. She can't touch you."

"Lenny bring me the bleach."

Lenny was still standing in the doorway watching to see what was going to happen. He went into the bathroom to retrieve the bleach and brought it to his mother in her room. She soon emerged and went into the children's room. She threw Sonya's uniforms on the floor and emptied the bottle of bleach on them.

"Go get your uniforms now," she smirked.

From the doorway, Sonya saw her uniforms laid out on the ground, covered in bleach and changing colour right before her eyes.

"Daddy it's fine. I don't need them. Come, let's go." Sonya stifled her tears.

"What do you mean you don't need them? You have to go sit your exams. She can't do anything to you. Take your things and come." He could tell that his daughter wanted to cry.

Lakresha went to stand by her sister and saw the uniforms covered in bleach. She pulled her sister by the hand into the room and showed her the suit of uniform she had hidden the night before. Sonya hugged her sister and cried. Lenny came in and the three kids helped her pack her things, including the books hiding under the bed beneath the floorboard. She whispered to them to keep all the money so they can use it to come see her. They would make a plan the first chance they got. Sonya made her mother no wiser. She wrapped up the bleached uniforms and stuffed them into a plastic bag. Nearing her father, he smelled the stench of the bleach and asked her to open the bag for him to see inside.

"You really bleached out the child's uniform? What is wrong with you? Do you want her to become nothing in life like you? That's your problem man, that's why you keep trying to kill them off. You ugly, jealous fool."

"Ugly like your mother. Jealous of them? They're just as ugly and worthless as you. I can't wait to get rid of them one by one."

"Let me take them then. Lenny and Lakresha, take your things and come. We will find a way to make it work. I won't leave you here with this mad witch."

"The only witch I know is your mother. Lenny and Lakresha won't leave this house and if you keep it up, I will call the police. Take your daughter and leave."

Sonya pulled on her father's shirt, "come daddy." She remembered the many times her father had had to spend the night in jail under the same circumstances. Her mother would call the police and lie that he'd hit her and they'd take him straight down to the lockup. She tugged at his shirt again.

"If God was like man, you would be dead you wicked woman. I don't know what kind of mother you are. You're a wicked witch; a wicked, ugly witch."

"Wicked, ugly witch just like your mother."

No one noticed Lakresha crying. She didn't want her sister to go but knew there was no alternative. Her mother had never thrown her out before. Lakresha knew she was serious. Her bleaching the uniforms was also very significant. Her punishments included going to school without lunch monies, ripping up their school books or even burning them but she'd never done anything so final. She seemed bent on not wanting Sonya to attend her exams. Kicking her out was also final and she seemed ready to cut all ties with Sonya. It also meant a lot for Lakresha and Lenny. There was no one in the house to protect them from their mother. As much as Sonya would also be attacked by her mother for defending her siblings, she'd always try to step in to shield them from her. They were on their own now.

Lenny walked through the back door and came into the front yard to hug his sister goodbye. Sonya left with her father.

The situation worsened for the two kids at home but especially for Lakresha. She was getting older and her mother wanted to ensure that she was not 'going to bring home a baby' in her teen years. She drove fear into Lakresha with both her words and actions.

When Lakresha got her period at 13, her mother gave her a feel of what sex would be like according to her. Lakresha went to her asking for pads, she locked her in her room alone. She soon returned with gloves on her hand and a bowl. She told Lakresha to lie on the floor with her legs open. Lakresha was surprised when her mother sat on her belly with her back towards her.

"Open your legs."

"No mommy, please," her eyes were burning from the fumes from the scotch bonnet peppers.

"Open your fucking legs now and don't make me angry. I keep telling you to stop talking to those boys. See now you have your periods. I'm not going to be a grandmother and you won't have a baby in this house. You need to feel what sex feels like so you'll take me seriously."

"Mommy, I'm not talking to any boys. I promise. I'm not going to have sex. Please mommy," Lakresha cried clamping her legs shut.

"Open your legs before you get it in your eyes. Open your legs!"

"Oh God no, I can't."

Her mother turned her upper body around just enough to run her gloved hand filled with pepper in Lakresha's eyes. It burned and Lakresha began to kick and scream. Her legs opened and her mother rubbed the pepper in her vagina. She dipped her hand into the bowl then rubbed the pieces of pepper in her vagina until the bowl was almost empty. She was thrown on the floor from Lakresha's kicking. Her vagina was on fire. Lakresha got up and ran to the bathroom, turning on the tap and washing the area but the burning wouldn't stop. Lenny heard his sister screaming and crying but stayed in their room. He was more afraid of their mother than any of the other kids. With no Sonya around to protect them he'd learned to stay out of his mother's way. He wanted to help his sister but didn't want to get his share of whatever she was getting, so instead of helping, he covered his head under his pillow and cried.

The next morning came and it was time for school. Lakresha spent the night getting up every so often to put ice or sugar on her vagina. It was swollen, burning and pained. Her mother came into the room to find out why Lakresha wasn't getting ready for school.

"I can't walk properly. I'm swollen." Lakresha turned to the wall, turning her back on her mother.

"Well at least you learned your lesson. I'm going to work now. Make sure the house is spotless when I get back."

Devon

Devon was the first of three children for his father but the only one for his mother. After their divorce, his mother was awarded custody of him and she won the family home as well. It was a five-bedroom mansion his parents were planning to raise a family in together. Those plans soon changed because Devon's father was a womaniser. He cheated on his wife one time too many and she finally asked for a divorce when she found out that another woman was having a child for him. He'd come home one day to find all his clothes in the front yard with cuts running through every single piece of them.

This was the first time Devon had seen such rage in his mother. She was usually very reserved and peaceful. When his mother told his father to leave and he'd driven away, Devon had chased after the car begging his father to take him. His father looked back at him through his rear-view mirror but didn't stop or slow down. His reality of having both parents in the home changed and now he'd only see his father every other weekend. The divorce was finalised just around his eight birthday.

Carla found it hard to cope after the divorce. She lost her job because of her constant drinking and turning up late for work. She barely ate. For dinner, she often had a full bottle of wine and was onto the next one by around 7pm each evening. She spent a lot of time in bed during the days and would hardly get up to look after Devon. He felt neglected but knew that his mother was having a hard time. Sometimes she drank so much she'd think that Devon was his father and would attack him. The most common thing was for her to chase him around the house with a knife, threatening to kill him. Devon would have to lock himself in a room to escape her.

One night Devon was sleeping when his mother climbed on top of him, threatening to stab him with a knife. He was only nine years old. Luckily, he woke up in time to fight her off. From then on, he'd always lock his door with the key before going to bed. That created its own problems too. When she couldn't get into his room, she'd try to kick the door in, keeping him awake as long as her body and the alcohol would allow. Sometimes it lasted into the wee hours of the morning. Some mornings Devon wouldn't be able to leave for school because she was outside the door threatening to kill him. He wanted to stay with his father full time but he worried about her too much and his step mother wasn't too fond of him either.

One Sunday afternoon his father dropped him off and for once she wasn't outside creating a scene. Devon went into the house to find her lying in her vomit on her bedroom floor. He dragged her in the shower and bathed her then cleaned the house. He wondered what would have happened if he hadn't come home. When would she finally get up and how long had she been lying there? He left her to sleep, wondering how his father could have left her and caused her to become like this. He became angry at both of them; his father for leaving and his mother for not pulling herself together and moving on the way he had.

In the middle of the night, his mother came beating down his door again.

"Dalton, open the door. I know you're in there with one of your women. Opennnnnnn!" she hammered the door. "Dalton! Open, we can have a threesome. I know you like freaky things, open the door."

She went away for a while and Devon imagined she'd probably not come back for the night. Not long after, she was right back at the door calling for his father to come out. "Dalton why did you close the door, come out! I'm going to chop you and the bitch you're in there with! Come out!"

"Mommy, daddy isn't in here. Go to your bed."

"Devon? Devon are you in there? Oh you're keeping secrets for your father. Open the door now!" She banged on the door hard.

Devon covered his head with the pillow, trying to block her out. But he could hear her banging on the door still. Eventually she gave up and went away. When he couldn't hear her anymore, he finally decided to sleep. It was already almost time to get up for school.

It had become a regular habit for him to fall asleep in class. He was always tired from the long nights he'd have putting up with his mother's antics.

"Devon, you're either missing my class or falling asleep in it. Are you working the night shift?" His teacher slapped him on the back of his head with her notebook.

"No Miss, I'm sorry."

"Well obviously I'm boring you. Didn't you sleep last night?"

"Not really Miss," Devon said without realising.

"What do you mean? What were you doing? I'm going to send you home with a letter to your mother. This is not the place for you to catch up on sleep. You're disturbing the lesson. Go wash your face and come back."

"Okay Miss."

Devon went to the bathroom to wash his face but didn't go back to class immediately. He sat on the toilet in one of the cubicles in the boy's bathroom and dosed off. He was feeling extremely fatigued. Suddenly he was awoken by a group of boys slamming the cubicle doors. For a brief moment he thought he was home. By the time he got back to class his teacher was teaching a different subject. She glared at him in the door way, completely annoyed.

"Just come in and sit down." She ushered him in.

By the age of 11, Devon's mother had sobered up and was back at work. She was a changed woman. She wasn't the quiet gentle mother he'd known. She started wearing very revealing clothes and brought home random men at nights; never the same one twice. One Sunday afternoon Devon walked into the kitchen to find his mother with a man on the counter. He tried running out of the room and was called back by his mother.

"Devon, come here." She could hear him going up the stairs. "Devon, don't let me have to come after you. Come here."

Devon raced to his room and locked himself in, pushing his chest of drawer behind the door for reinforcement. He could hear his mother making sexual noises in the kitchen. He turned on his TV and turned it all the way up. Devon laid across his bed and placed his pillow over his head, trying to escape from his reality.

A few days later, in the middle of the night, Devon's mother finally came home with a man he'd never seen before, after he'd been waiting on his own for hours. He was worried sick and waited for her in the hall way. Realising she was alive and well, Devon began to climb the stairs to go to his room. His mother dragged him by his shirt and he stumbled backwards, holding on to the railing to catch his balance. He tried to shake his mother off him but she held on to his shirt and kept pulling him.

"What are you doing? Leave the boy alone."

"No he likes to watch. He's going to watch."

"What, who is he? You didn't say anything about that."

"It's okay, you'll enjoy it too."

"Obviously he doesn't want to watch, otherwise he wouldn't be fighting you off. He's only a boy, leave him alone."

"Just shut up. Let me handle this."

"Girlfriend you're cute and everything, but I didn't sign up for this. I don't like the 'kids thing'. So guess what, I'll catch you some other time; better yet, have a good life." He walked out of the house, slamming the door behind him.

Devon's mother pranced on him and bit him in his neck. He tried to shake her off but she wouldn't let go. He could feel her teeth sinking deeper and deeper into his flesh.

"Stop man!" with all his might, he pushed her off him and she went rolling down the bottom of the stairs. Devon held on to his neck which was now burning and climbed the steps to his bedroom. As usual he locked himself in his room away from his mother. Downstairs, he could hear her crying. He was trying hard not to fall for it, but he couldn't help himself.

"Mommy, why are you crying?"

"Don't ask me anything. You pushed me down. You're just like your good for nothing whoring father. You're going to beat women, you damn dog." She got up from the kitchen stool with a knife in her hand, backing him against the wall. She choked him with one hand and pressed the knife into his belly. "One of these days I will push it all the way in." She twisted the knife.

Devon stared into the ceiling at nothing. He was used to this. When she realised he wasn't reacting, she dropped the knife and fell to the ground whaling.

"You don't love me. I know you only care about your father. You want to go live with him. I know you want to leave me."

"Mommy stop the foolishness. I'm not going anywhere. I'm always going to stay here with you."

"You're only saying that now. I know you're planning to leave. You don't like me. I know you don't love me either."

"Mommy calm down." Devon bent to pick his mother up off the floor and hugged her limp body. He knew she was only trying to get his attention but either way he wanted her to stop crying. "Let's watch some TV." He walked her into the living room. She fell asleep in the middle of the movie and Devon was finally able to catch a nap.

"What's wrong with your belly? It's all blue."

"It's nothing. I think it's from PE last week. Don't worry about it."

"We didn't have PE last week remember. Mr Reid wasn't here. Doesn't it hurt?"

"No it doesn't. I don't know how it happened but it really doesn't hurt, that's why I didn't realise it was there. Come on let's go out before Sir gives us extra laps for being late."

"Okay, let's go but you should really get the bruises seen to. It looks really bad."

"I will," Devon lied. "Ryan, please don't say anything to anyone. I promise I will sort it."

"Okay, I won't. Let's go."

Devon struggled to get through PE. He was in severe pain. His ribs and back were aching. Two days before, him and his mother had gotten into a fight or rather she'd attacked him in his sleep. He came home from school and was home alone. He was exhausted. He fell asleep on the sofa. At first he thought he was dreaming, then he realised that someone was really on top of him. He opened his eyes to see his mother straddling him and unbuttoning her blouse.

"Mommy, what are you doing?"

"Just lay down, don't worry. You look just like your father. You're becoming a man now: all grown up."

"Mommy stop it. Get off me," Devon shuffled.

"Stay still. There's no need to be shy. Come on, give me your hands."

"Mommy! Get off me!"

"Who the hell do you think you're talking to?" She leaned over and wrapped her hand around his throat. "Don't you dare talk to me like that ever."

Devon mustered up all his strength and threw his mother off her. He climbed over the arm of the sofa to get away from her and she got up and wrestled him to the floor. She punched him in his ribs repeatedly then held on to his penis and twisted it. Devon screamed in anguish. She got up off him and stepped in his penis area, pushing her foot down further and further.

"You're just like your fucking worthless father; just as fucking ugly," she kicked him. "I hate you. I'm tired of seeing your fucking face every single day." She kicked him again. Devon turned his back to her, trying to shield himself from her. "You're just like your fucking father!" She kicked him again. She started crying. When she'd had enough, she went to the fridge to grab herself a glass of orange juice, leaving Devon on the floor. He was only 13 years old.

"Was that your mother again?"

"Yeah, I really think I should go over and make sure she's okay."

"Devon, you can't keep doing this. I can't keep doing this with you and you can't keep doing this to our family. When will you break free from her? You have to stop letting her do this to you."

"She's my mother Jessica, I can't turn my back on her. She needs me."

"When is she going to be there for you? She does this because she knows she'll get away with it. What's the problem now?"

"I don't know. I could barely hear what she'd saying. She's just crying. I don't think she's okay."

"Devon, I love you and I want to be there for you but I really can't keep doing this. You keep running back to her for her to break you then you come back with more problems I can't fix. What about your own son Devonte? Do you want him to have to deal with this too? You need to focus on yourself and getting right. Your mother knows the hold she has on you and no matter what she does to you, you will be there for her. When are you going to stop her?"

Devon didn't know what to do. He knew that his wife was right but he didn't know how to not care about his mother. He was all she really had. Sure she could call her sister or one of her friends, but she called him and that meant she needed him. He knew that he'd go there and it would be the same old story and he'd be having nightmares for consecutive nights but he needed to make sure she was okay.

"Daddy, are you okay?"

He saw his little face look up at him and got his answer. He needed to be there for his own child the way his mother never was for him.

"I'm okay, Daddy's okay." A tear fell from his eye. He reached down to pick his son up, threw him on his neck and went outside to play with him.

Amoy

I was passed around so much in my young life. At the age of six years old I was sent to live with my aunt who had two teenage daughters but was soon pawned off when one of my teenage cousins fell pregnant, causing my aunt a lot of stress. My aunt sent me to live with my grandmother in another Parish. I remember a good life with her. Until then I'd not yet been to school, although most Jamaican children started school from the early age of two or three.

I remember my grandmother begging a teacher in the community to accept me in school and she did. She didn't have much; she used some old fabric she had in the house to make my uniform, which looked nothing like the prescribed uniform. But I was overjoyed as she had taken interest in me and my wellbeing. I couldn't read and I constantly worried that my teacher would call me in front of the class to read and would beat me when she realised I couldn't call the words on the page, as she had done with other children. It seemed though that she was aware of my circumstances, so she never did. One afternoon, after school had ended and I was heading home, she called me back and gave me a story book to take home. I remember thinking how pretty the book was and feeling sad that I didn't know how to call the words on the page; but I was determined to learn.

While my grandmother did the chores in the house, I walked around behind her constantly nagging her, asking her for help. She'd always know the words and help me break them into syllables for me to learn them. Before long, I was reading. I was seven in grade two and at the end of the school year I was placed third in my class of 46 children. This was my very first accomplishment and my grandmother was just happy as I were. She wanted to keep me in school.

My grandmother begged my father to buy the right fabric to make my school uniform, but he was not interested. Therefore, I kept going to school standing out like a sore thumb. I looked different from everyone. I had no self-confidence. I felt odd; but I had a deep desire inside me to learn. Then by the end of grade three, my father would come to dampen that spirit.

"Errol, glad you finally decide to come by my son," my grandmother called out to my father walking into the unpaved front yard.

"Mommy what is it now? The only time you're glad to see me is when you want something, so what is it now?"

"Boy, I don't want anything from you. I work make my own money and take care of myself. But you must remember you have a child here who have needs. The child is doing well in school and...."

"Mommy, I can't even come into the yard properly without you starting all this foolishness." My father spoke with contempt.

"Don't raise your voice in this yard. You have responsibilities. I raised you better. Amoy doing well in school but she cannot continue wearing that uniform. The principal not very happy. Every day they send home another note."

"What's wrong with what she's wearing now?"

"It shows you know nothing about this child. The uniform must be blue and she's wearing orange because that's all the fabric I can find in the house. I can't afford to pay fare, plus go buy the uniform material. I don't have enough money. I made the uniforms from she got here, it's almost two years now. I have a blue skirt I can cut but it can't make a full uniform: I really don't know what else to do."

"Mommy, mommy, enough of this now. I'm taking her to her mother so stop wasting time. She won't need any uniforms."

"What you mean taking her back to her mother? Leave the child where she is. How can a man find it hard to give to his own child? What in the heaven's name is wrong with you boy?"

I heard the conversation from behind the front door, where I was hiding. I wanted to scare my father when he entered the house but hearing that he was "sending me" to my mother made me sad. Once again, I was being pawned off, like nothing. I didn't know my mother and I had longed to lay eyes on the woman that had created me but I was happy with my grandmother, who was nurturing and kind hearted. My teacher showed me love and kindness and I was happy. I didn't want to leave.

After grade three ended and summer passed, I was still with my grandmother. The new school year started and my father had not been back to visit or take me to my mother as he had promised my grandmother. I spent the entire first term of what was supposed to be grade four, carrying water from the standpipe with my grandmother and reading all the books I could lay hands on. I read some of them so much that I remembered them word for word, for pages on end. Then one day, a teacher turned up at my house unannounced.

"Ms Miriam? Hello?" she had called out behind the makeshift gate made out of bits of tree branches.

"Who's that?" My grandmother emerged from the backyard where she had been plucking chickens. This was how she earned a living. She raised chickens and sold them on to the people in our neighbourhood.

"It's me Mrs Campbell from school. I'm here about Amoy."

"Oh, hello Teacher. How you doing?"

"Good Ms Miriam, yourself?"

"I'm good my child, give God thanks. Just busy 'round the back doing some work to get ready for the weekend sale."

"Aw Ms Miriam, you're always busy at work," she smiled.

"I have to do what I can Teacher, mouths to feed and bills to pay. I can't just sit around and do nothing. But come, let's go inside and talk." The two of them climbed the front step and sat on the veranda. "Amoy, bring some water for Teacher."

"I don't want to take up too much of your time, so I'll try to be brief. Ms Miriam, why did Amoy stop coming to school?"

"You know this is my son's child and I'm keeping her here with me for him. I keep begging him to get the uniform so the child can go to school but the boy refuse no matter how much I beg. Then he told me he's taking the child back to her mother but to this day the boy can't come and take her. I know she needs school but with the little I have my priority is to make sure she eats and can live. I cannot afford the uniform teacher."

"I understand Ms Miriam but you shouldn't keep her at home. She's a smart girl. She was doing so well. Tell you what. If he doesn't come and take her by next month after the new year, then send her. I will talk to the principal and let him allow her in what she has."

"Teacher, Amoy can't wear those uniforms again. She grew them out. One of them look like miniskirt and the other one have a big banana stain in it. She doesn't even have clothes I could send her in. What she wears in the yard is from what I make by patching different bits of my own clothes together for her."

"Okay Ms Miriam, I will see what I can do. Don't you worry. I will come back to see whether the father has taken her, then we can go from there."

As customary, I was not allowed to be in the room while the adults were speaking but I heard every word from the front room. I was happy to hear this.

January came and my father never took me to my mother as I had then come to expect. Mrs Campbell kept her word and came to the house for a follow up. She brought three uniforms with her the Sunday before the first day of the school term in January. On Monday morning, my grandmother dressed me in the uniform and shoes she had brought. I was so proud and happy. I was going back to school and I was wearing the same things as the other children. They were second hand uniform but to me they could have very well been made out of gold.

I had missed so much of school; it had a huge impact. I struggled to catch up with the class and at the end of the school year I was only four places from the last place in the class of 45. My confidence took a big hit. I was disappointed in myself. I felt defeated.

The following year came and I continued at the same school. Within days of starting grade five, my grandmother suddenly had to move from the neighbourhood and once again I was out of school. The first few weeks I watched the neighbourhood children made their way to school with grave jealousy. A neighbour soon helped my grandmother to get me into a new school.

Missing so much school had its disadvantages. I struggled to keep up and could hardly manage the syllabus. But I was willing to put the effort in. I just wanted to settle down and have a normal school life, like most of the other kids.

In the middle of the term, my grandmother uprooted us again and we moved back into her old house in our old neighbourhood. I couldn't be angry with her because she'd moved for our own safety. One of my uncles had gotten into trouble with other men from the neighbourhood, who continued to make trouble for my grandmother. We had to move.

Coming back, my grandmother gave me a letter to take to my old grade five teacher. Dressed in my old uniforms I made my way to school. I felt terrible that my grandmother hadn't taken me herself. I felt uncomfortable. It was late in the morning as well when she'd sent me off. Making my way, I wondered whether they'd accept me back in school and whether I'd have to walk back home in the dreadful sun alone and disappointed.

Arriving at the grade five classroom, I stood waiting outside, armed with my letter in hand. I was filled with shame and couldn't raise my head to look the teacher in her eye. I could feel the entire class glaring at me. She must have sensed how terrible I was feeling.

"Come in Amoy. There's a seat over there, go in and sit down."

She didn't take my letter or asked for an explanation.

I was happy to be back among familiar faces.

In the same school year there was yet more disruption in my life. My father finally turned up one day and took me to live with him. At my grandmother's request, he decided to let me finish the school year. Though this was good, staying in school, it was physically daunting. Getting to school meant taking three taxis each way and I had to learn this all on my own.

It was a new and different life for me. My stepmother who lived with my father and my younger sister took no interest in me. It was my father who combed my hair, prepared my meals and did pretty much everything for me. My stepmother would leave me without food when my father was at work and he'd come home late at nights to a hungry crying child.

Soon my father who was a mechanic would start taking me with him to work and this became overwhelming for him. On some nights, where he hadn't made enough for the day, he would have to sleep in town and this meant I also had to sleep in town. He never had a car so we'd often have to sleep in an old abandoned car on the empty lot next to the garage he worked at. I could tell it was hard for him and he was struggling with all of this.

One evening, my aunt who I'd lived with when I was six years old came to pick me up. My father explained that I would stay with her and she'd take me back in the morning to go to school. He didn't want me to have to sleep with him on the street anymore because it was dangerous. Then it became routine. I knew when my father hadn't made enough because he'd walk me to the bus park to meet my aunt, who would take me home with her. It was no bed of roses staying with her, but it was a far cry better than being at my father's house with just my stepmother, who treated me like nothing short of garbage. At this young stage in my life I knew my life was rough.

Out of the blue, one weekend, my father packed my bag with the few pieces of clothes I owned and writing books. We left the house together and when I arrived at my grandmother's house I was relieved.

"Mama, mama!" I ran and jumped into her arms, almost toppling her over.

"What a sight this bright Saturday morning? Errol? How you doing?"

"I'm alright Mama."

"Errol what is this?" She questioned my father.

"I brought her to say goodbye to you mommy. Taking her to her mother because I can't manage. She needs some motherly guidance. She's getting big now."

"She's been big Errol and what do you mean you can't manage? What about Nadine, she's not there anymore?"

"She's at the house but you know how that goes."

"Hm, ah boy. Alright."

I remember my grandmother giving me some coins, telling me to take care of myself and not forget her. My father and I travelled on a bus for what seems like days then we took a taxi and arrived outside a house I'd not been to before. There was a man there with a small child. I soon realised the man was my step-father and the child my sister. My father explained that I'd be living with my mother from then on.

I remember feeling nervous inside my stomach, eager to meet her for the first time. I didn't want an explanation as to why she was never around. As young as I was, I imagined she had no choice but to leave me and I couldn't hold it against her. I just wanted to meet her. My father left before my mother came home. It was getting late and he had to get back home. I knew I would miss him, but my emotions were selfishly reserved for my mother. I wanted to lay eyes on her.

It got dark and finally my mother came home. I was so happy to see her.

"Wait what is this?" she said, arriving in the living room.

"Errol dropped her off. I don't really know what is going on. He only said she's staying with you now, nothing else."

She hissed her teeth and threw her handbag down on the sofa next to me, "Errol will come and get her. There's no space here. Where will she sleep? I'm struggling as it is."

"Evelyn say hi to the child at least," my stepfather demanded, "deal with everything else after."

"Johnny, I don't have time for any of this. Mama see her yet? What am I really supposed to do with this now? Tell me." She went into her bedroom, slamming the door.

No one was happy to see me; not my sister living with my mother, my older sister living upstairs with my grandmother or my own mother. But something inside me was just overjoyed. I was in the same place as my mother, even if she didn't want me there.

In the end, my mother gave up trying to get my father to come collect me and my grandmother gave me a place next to my older sister on her single bed. My sister was hateful and directed all that hate towards me. Sometimes in the middle of the night she'd use her foot to force me off the bed and I'd be startled from falling on the floor. She hated sharing anything with me and I believe she found it difficult to even share a kind word. I felt unwelcomed and out of place but I was still happy to be able to see my mother every day.

My mother kept promising to get me into the primary school, walking distance from the house, but kept delaying taking me to be registered. Every morning, I'd wake up with my older sister preparing to go to school, slamming everything around us just to wake me up. My mother would call out for me when she was up and I'd go downstairs to begin my chores. It was a long list of chores, not like anything I was accustomed to.

Each morning I'd first have to make the bed my mother and stepfather slept in. Then I'd have to empty and wash their chamber pot, wait for it to dry then replace it under their bed. I would then have to sweep the house and wash up the dishes. My breakfast would be whatever was left in the pot from the night before or what my mother had left for me after they'd have breakfast. The most common would be a piece of yam or potato left in the pot from the night before or a slice of bread left on the counter.

Eventually, she'd got me into school as promised. But the torture continued. I would still have to do all the chores in her house every morning before leaving for school and she'd only give me enough money for a small pack of biscuit. It wasn't enough for a proper meal. Sometimes, I'd walk home at lunchtime to scrummage for whatever I could find but after walking back so many times and coming up empty and having to walk back to school on a hungry stomach, I decided to start bearing the hunger at school every day. I didn't want anyone to know that I was without lunch at school so at the ring of the bell, I'd hide away until it was time for class again.

My new school was academically relaxed compared to the two schools I'd been to previously. It was time to prepare for GSAT and I knew that I was not prepared. I started to collect text books, whichever ones I could get my hand on, in preparation. I decided that I'd teach myself what I didn't know and prepare as best as I could. I'd learned enough by then to know that I wanted to achieve an education.

One evening I was outside in the yard studying from a Religious Education book a teacher at school loaned me to use. I noticed my mother walking into the yard but I was so engulfed in the book that I didn't rush to serve her as I usually would.

"Wait, am I invisible? Don't you see me?"

"No mommy," I jumped up from the building block I was sitting on and followed her into her house with my book in hand.

"What is that in your hand?"

"It's an RE book mommy. My teacher lend it to me so I can study for GSAT. I want to go to Ardenne mommy, teacher says if I study hard I can go."

She hissed her teeth, "Ardenne, the way you missed school you won't pass a thing. As a matter of fact, the only school you will pass for is Edith and be happy because that's the only uniform you'll look good in anyway. Pass me the flour from the cupboard."

I wanted to cry hearing her say that. I knew it was going to be a hard task even passing GSAT and wanted some form of reassurance from her as my mother. My grandmother had done the best with what she had and she didn't have much but she always encouraged and helped me with doing better in school. It was not only different to see how I was being treated by my mother, it was also hurtful. I made up my mind to block her out and work hard to pass GSAT.

Exams came and passed and then finally the results were out. I had gotten placed at my second choice of school. No one had congratulated me on passing. I had beaten all the odds and done my absolute best and got placed in a top high school but no one seemed happy for me. Immaculate was a new and different ball game for me. I was unhappy.

I had to take two buses to go to school and I was only given my fare with no lunch money or lunch to take with me. At first, I hid it well but then I was relived when I realised that I didn't have to hide it, as there were other girls like me at school who also had no support or lunch for school. One girl wouldn't even be given money for bus fare for school. In both support and economical strategy, we all walked to Half-Way Tree after school in the afternoons. We would then be able to save the extra bus fare to pool our monies together on Fridays to treat ourselves to lunch. This wasn't guaranteed every Friday though, as most times none of us had the money.

By the eight-grade, life at home worsened. My mother had another child who was living with her father who was dropped off the same way I was. This meant my mother had two younger children at home needing care. Both her and my stepfather worked so they were my responsibility.

My older sister was stronger and tougher than I was. She never really had a relationship with my mother. It was my grandmother who supported her financially and provided to her needs. Therefore, it was all up to me to help my mother look after my younger sisters.

She was kind to them and expected me to be the same but resentment grew inside me. They were well fed. Everyday I would have to drop them off at school, before making my own way to school and my mother always ensured their lunch kit were packed with lunch and extra snacks. I was often tempted to rob them of some of their snacks but was always reminded of how hunger felt and didn't want them to experience that.

My life was full of fear. If I didn't do something properly, picked up my sisters a minute too late, didn't wash every piece of clothing in the house on Saturday mornings or even stood in a place my mother didn't want me to; I was beaten. I had to make sure that I was outside waiting for them when their school ended, which was difficult as my own school was almost an hour away by bus and more with walking the first journey from school. It meant that I was beaten almost every single day. I was always scared: always on my guard ready to take whatever she'd do to me. When I cleaned the house, my mother would walk around to inspect the work. If something wasn't done the way she wanted me to, she'd ask me whether it was done properly, then before I could even answer or correct it, she'd start banging my head into the wall. Sometimes it would split open and bleed, or I'd just end up with a lump.

My grandmother passed on and both me and my older sister had to move in with my mother full time. They didn't get along. She had no regard for my mother. I suppose my sister was grieving because she started sleeping out and would show up whenever she pleased. She was only 15 and whenever she returned, she and my mother would be arguing for hours, until one of them left the house again. One Saturday morning, my mother gave me fare and told me to go collect money from my father as she didn't have the money to send me to school the following week. I didn't know if I was going to find my father but I was willing to make the journey anyway. I wanted some peace away from the argument and nonstop work. I was always busy with chores and taking care of my siblings. I needed a break.

"Kerry, Amoy is going to her father, you need to look after the babies today until I get back from the market."

"Look after which babies? I don't have any kids, I'm going out."

I didn't wait to hear the rest of the conversation between my mother and older sister. I hurried to the bathroom, washed my face and brushed my teeth quickly. I didn't shower. I slipped into the only pair of jeans I had and grabbed a grey top my father had sent me, grabbed my school shoes and slipped out the back door. I could hear the two arguing but I wasn't going to turn around to be kept back to watch my siblings.

I convinced my father to let me stay until the following day. Upon returning, I heard murmurs in the lane that my sister had left home. Getting into the house my mother was still arguing and this time her anger was directed at me. She claimed my sister and I were plotting against her and wanted to take over her house. Looking around our room,

I saw nothing in sight belonging to my sister and realised that she was really gone: not for the night or two as she normally was, this time all her belongings were gone with her. I felt a rush of sadness because although she didn't like me, it helped having her around to bear some of my mother's wrath. With her gone, I was now all alone and everything would be directed at me. I had to bear it too: unlike my sister, I didn't have anywhere to go so I had to take whatever she threw at me. Rebelling was not an option.

Then my mother had another baby.

The summer before going into grade nine is one I remember quite well. With the new baby, I now had three small children to care for during the day on top of pretty much running a house, making sure it was clean from top to bottom as my mother liked it. When they left for work, they only left food for the small children; baby porridge and formula, plus snacks for the two older ones. They would purposely not leave anything for me to eat. One morning while my step father was getting dressed for work, I asked him to leave something with me to eat. I knew my mother kept the groceries in her room which he would lock when he was leaving, so I wanted him to leave me something before going. I wouldn't usually ask as I figured they'd leave me food just as they did the younger ones if they cared. To my surprise, he dipped into his pocket and left me $300. I felt relieved that he understood my plight. I happily bought flour and tin mackerel, as I planned to have enough for as long as possible.

"Evlyn, this little girl has no shame. This morning she created one big disgrace in the road telling everyone how you leave her here without food. She's a disgrace."

I was shocked to hear him say this. It was a blatant lie. My mother reached for me, collaring me in the front of my blouse and started punching me in my head. She kept punching and punching, I couldn't hear what she was saying but I knew she was quarrelling. She kept punching me in almost the exact same spot. It felt as though my head was about to explode so I turned, trying to give her a new place to punch but her fist came down and punched my tooth. My mother got so mad, she pulled me to the kitchen and used the frying pan to beat me where ever on my body it connected. I couldn't even cry. That day and many subsequent ones made me realise that my step father was just as evil was my mother. He never raised a hand to me but he was always quick to give my mother a reason to try to kill me and never ever tried to step in and tell my mother to stop, no matter how bad things got.

When I was in high school I left for school through the back door. I thought I closed the door behind me as I normally would but I hadn't. My step father got home before me and told my mother when she got home that he came home to find the back door opened. My mother got a big piece of wood and beat me so badly with it I still have scars on my body from it. I remember the flesh between my middle and ring finger on my left hand splitting open you could see the soft white flesh coming out. The cut ran from between the fingers down into my palm. It obviously needed stitches but no one cared. The same night my mother made me do the dishes and it was so painful I couldn't even hold anything with it. I still had to get my siblings ready for school in the morning plus clean the house. My entire body was sore. I remember taking too long in the bathroom because I was crying. When I went to school I couldn't sit down comfortably because I was in so much pain.

To be honest my 'childhood' was just rough.

I remember when I was 19 my mother woke me early in the morning to get the three kids ready for school. I bathed them, fed them and dressed them as usual. We were ahead of schedule so I had time to do the dishes before walking them to school. While in the kitchen, I could hear my mother arguing outside. No one was out there with her, she was quarrelling about what she was going to do to me if everything wasn't done by the time she got home. I was busy job hunting and had gone into town the previous day for an interview so I didn't have time to wash some clothes she'd asked me to wash.

"Mommy, why are you so fussy? I'm going to do it today."

She came back into the house immediately, "what did you just say?"

"You don't need to be so miserable, I'm going……" She threw a ceramic mug at me, hitting me in the back of my head. It sounded like my scull cracked open. I felt the warmth of the blood trailing down my back.

"Look what you made me did. Now I'll have to take off work to take you to the doctor."

"Take to which doctor? Let her figure it out herself. Put on your shoes and go to work." My step father advised.

My mother hissed her teeth, went to the veranda, slipped into her work shoes and left for work.

I couldn't stop the bleeding so I decided to go to the hospital. The doctor kept asking me what had happened, but I was too ashamed to tell her. She threatened to call he police and I finally told her.

"Is your mother going through any form of bereavement or anything like that?" she asked.

"Doctor, this is mild. My mother is always like this sometimes worse."

"What do you mean worse? Has she done other things like this to you?"

"I don't want to talk about it. One day hopefully I'll find a job and move out, then it will stop."

"You know, your mother is either going through something or she's crazy. This isn't normal and it isn't okay."

I almost laughed. "Well she must be crazy or she's always been going through something because she'd always been like this.

The doctor shaved out the hair from around the cut and gave me seven stitches. I had a bald spot on my head and my hair was short so it was obvious. I couldn't hide it. I had an interview the day after and lied when the interviewer asked me what had happened. I told her I got the cut from a fall and told her I didn't want to talk about it. I never told anyone the truth about it for a very long time, not even my closest friends. I was ashamed.

When I was 20, one of my aunts took me in. I finally got a job. I had to leave while my mother was at work. She didn't want me to work because she wouldn't have anyone to help her with the children. She would refuse to give me taxi fare to go to my interviews. I was determined to find a job that would enable me to save to send myself to college. I couldn't just sit around being a nanny and continue to depend on the mercy of my neighbours for food.

My aunt was a single mother with a teenage son and couldn't afford to help me financially. She allowed me to stay with her rent free plus gave me a loan for lunch and taxi fare for the first couple of weeks of work. She was kind to me, even though she didn't have much herself. She was motherly.

Over the years the relationship between me and my mother continued to break down. I would make an effort to have a relationship with her then she'd throw it back in my face by betraying my trust every single time. The sad part is that I know that my mother can do better as a mother, the way she's done for my younger sisters. She's never raised a hand to any of them and the three of them together wouldn't know how to make a bed because they've never had to do it, let alone clean an entire house, wash six people's clothes, nonstop ironing and everything else I had to do. Even today my mother still treats me poorly.

I used to want her love and approval so bad I'd put up with anything in hope that one day she'd love me or even be kind towards me. I've given up on that now. If at thirty-five years old I haven't achieved that and every chance she gets she tries to tear me down, there's no hope of things ever changing.

I've given up. I am the child and it's time she tried being the mother.

Barrington

Barrington was the middle child. His parents had two children together; him and his older sister. His mother had his younger brother Carl with her partner after their father. Carl's father left shortly after his mother got pregnant so Carl doesn't know or have a relationship with him. Barrington and his sister Brandy were extremely close: inseparable. They were only two years apart. Their younger brother on the other hand, being much younger and sickly, was always cloaked up by his mother. He had a hole in his heart which made his mother very protective of him. She wouldn't let him out of her sight.

Barrington loved his mother no matter what she did to him, there was no one in the world like her to him. In his eyes, she was the one who made things right in their not so wonderful world. Whatever she did to him he'd write it off as her having a bad day or him causing it on himself. After his father, left things had gotten bad for her. She couldn't afford to feed them. Their electricity and water were both almost always cut off and the landlord would always be at their door trying to get his rent from his mother who would be hiding inside telling them to be quiet. She kept a tab with both shops in their neighbourhood and often went too far past her payment dates and amounts to get more credit. She'd often send one of the older kids with a letter to the shopkeeper, who'd send them back empty handed to her. They really didn't have much.

Things got better for them for a short while when Carl's father just started coming around then got sour once he'd up and left just like their own father had. Barrington and his sister went to a school in the neighbourhood. The teachers knew they both came to school without food and would often find a way to feed them. Although in Barrington's eyes his mother was an angel, that wasn't the reality.

She showed no pity when she disciplined her two older children. Whatever she could get her hands on would do the trick. Barrington himself has been beaten with hoses, electrical wires, knives, machetes, pipelines and have even been stoned by his mother on several occasions.

He was only six or seven years old when his mother tied him to a tree in their yard and stoned him. He'd taken off in the morning with some of the neighbourhood boys and spent the day roaming the streets, playing all day. She called for him and even sent Brandy to search for him but couldn't find him. When he got home she was fuming. She dragged him outside into the yard and tied him to the tree. She refused to hit him with her hands, claiming she didn't want to hurt her herself. Earlier in the day she'd told Brandy to fill a bucket with rocks. She sat on a tree stump about a metre away from him and stoned him. When the stones were finished and Barrington was crying, she called Brandy to pick up the stones and refill the bucket. Brandy cried for her brother as she reluctantly filled the bucket with the stones.

"Mommy, please stop. You're going to kill him. He won't do it again."

"Don't get involved before you end up right next to him."

"Mommy he's not going to do it again."

"Bring the rest of the stones to me and don't aggravate me."

Brandy stopped picking up the stones and threw her body onto her brother's to shield him. Her mother stoned them both.

"Untie him. The two of you pick up the stones and come inside when you're finished. I bet you won't go away all day again. You give too much problems, you damn little ugly boy." She went inside.

Brandy untied her brother and walked him over to the stump his mother had vacated and helped him to sit down.

"I'm going to pick up the stones. Wait here for me."

"Your head is bleeding."

"It's fine. I'm fine."

"Poochie, tell Barrington to give me my money."

"Which money?"

"The $3000 he took out of my house."

"Barrington," she bellowed for him, "come here now."

"Yes mommy."

"Where's Jackie's $3000?"

"Huh, which $3000 mommy? She didn't give me any money."

"I didn't give it to you. You stole it out of my house this morning."

"I didn't come into your house and I didn't take your money."

"Shut up. Where did you put the money?" His mother questioned.

"Mommy I didn't take any money. I didn't go into her house this morning."

"You're too damn thief. Go get the money and bring it to me."

"But mommy I don't have the money. I didn't take it." Barrington felt embarrassed. "I'm not a thief."

"I know you took the money, Eddy saw you come into my house this morning. Just bring my money and don't make me angry. It's my money to send my kids to school."

"Barrington, where is the money? Get it and bring it to me now. I won't beat you."

"Mommy I didn't take anyone's money. Eddy didn't see me do anything because I never left the house this morning. You know I didn't leave the house."

"I don't know anything. Don't pull me into it with you."

"Mommy he never left the house. We've been cleaning our room."

"Brandy you like taking your brother's side even when he's wrong."

"He didn't take your money. Leave him alone."

"You, shut up and go inside now. Barrington, do not let me have to ask you for the money again. Stop embarrassing me."

"Mommy you're the one embarrassing yourself. I didn't take the money."

"Watch your mouth before I knock out your teeth."

"I didn't take her money. Eddy is lying. Maybe he took the money now he's looking for a scapegoat."

"Hey, fucking ugly boy, don't accuse my child. I'll slap you in your face."

"Then tell him to stop telling lies. What is he hiding?"

"Shut up man. Shut up and bring the woman's money to her now. Brandy bring the belt."

"Mommy I can't bring money I don't have. Where must I get $3000?"

"Poochie, if he doesn't give me my money I'm calling the police now. Tell him to give me my money."

"There's no need to call the police," she collared Barrington and started punching him. "Give, the, woman, her, money." Each word followed by a pause and a punch to his face. She kept beating him but he didn't hand over the money. He couldn't have either because he hadn't stolen it.

Days later they'd find out that Jackie's own son had taken the money. The other kids were treated to biscuits and sodas the entire weekend. It was when Lilly heard that Barrington was accused, that she realised what had happened. She told her mother about the treats Eddy had bought for the gang and she knew immediately that he'd taken the money. The adults discussed it but neither Jackie nor his own mother apologised to him for accusing him of stealing the money. He felt ashamed that his mother had thought of him as a thief but didn't hold it against her.

She accused him many more times in his life of stealing but Barrington held himself in high esteem. Unlike his mother, he never begged or borrowed from anyone. He believed that if he didn't have, he would do without. Stealing from someone else was not something he found ethical.

By the ninth grade, things at home had gotten worse for Barrington and he started acting out at school. He wasn't the smartest kid in school. He needed more attention that the average learner and teachers didn't have that to offer.

He was barely making average pass marks in his subjects and only excelled in building technology, which he really liked. He was naturally good with his hands. Building technology needed tools his mother refused to buy. She didn't see the need for children to be sent home with a book list that included anything outside of a couple of notebooks and pens for school. Everything else, according to her, was a rip off to the parents who had to purchase them. She refused to purchase any of the tools and soon he gave up on that subject as well. He grew tired of being kicked out of class for not having the right materials and started hiding away from classes.

In the middle of ninth grade, he was kicked out of school once and for all.

In the morning, Barrington was beaten by his mother when he asked for taxi fare to go to school and she refused claiming that he was a dunce and didn't need to go to school that day. Barrington told her that he's not a dunce and that he was only failing school because she refused to take care of her responsibilities which meant he had to suffer the consequences. She punched him and beat him, ripping the buttons off his shirt. He picked up another shirt he had ironed and walked to his uncle who worked not far from their house. He gave him taxi fare and lunch money to go to school. He was still upset when he arrived at school and sat in a corner in the class ignoring everyone. The geography teacher came into the classroom and asked for everyone to take their seat and started the class. Barrington stared down at the drawing he was making on the inside cover of his notebook and did not acknowledge the teacher who took notice.

"Why did you throw the duster at me?" Barrington shifted just in time the duster missed his head.

"Didn't you see me come in? Didn't you hear me come in?"

"Tell me something, is there something on my face that says "beating stick"?

"Who do you think you're talking to?"

"I'm asking you. Do I look like a beating stick? Do you think I'm just here to be beaten and treated like shit by everybody? What if I took up the duster and hit you with it? How would you feel?"

The teacher grabbed her books and ran out of the classroom. Moments later two security guards and the principal came to the classroom.

"Barrington Dailey?"

Barrington didn't answer. He gazed out the window, pretending not to hear his principal calling his name.

"Barrington Dailey?" He patted him on his shoulder, "don't you hear me calling you?"

Barrington looked up at him, "yes Sir?"

"Why are you threatening your teacher?"

"That's what she told you yeah; that I threatened her." Barrington tried to get up to walk away.

"Young man sit down until I say you can get up," he forced him back on the chair by his shoulder.

"Sir, it's fine. Anyone who is honest in this classroom can tell you that I didn't threaten her. I asked her a question.

Everyday everybody just get up and beat and illtreat me. She threw the duster at me so I asked her how she would feel if I threw the duster at her. We are all humans no matter how young we are. But it's fine. You came up here with your security guards. I don't want to be beaten up and end up in jail so let me rather go. It's fine."

"Young man, relax."

"Sir why are you telling me to relax. I'm not raising my voice. I'm not doing anything to you but it seems you also want to tell lies on me."

The whole class went "Ohhhh", in unison. They were all shocked.

"Mr Spence, walk this young man to the front gate. Don't come back without a parent. Tell your mother or father to come and pick up a letter. They need to find you a new school."

"Okay Sir." Barrington walked with the security guard, who ushered him out the main gate.

His mother only realised he'd not been going to school after a few weeks. She almost beat him to death but it was nothing he wasn't used to.

Levy, a man in the neighbourhood, took a liking to Barrington. He worked in construction. When he noticed that Barrington wasn't going to school anymore, he took him under his wing and taught him the trade. Barrington was only 15 when he started working. Every week when Barrington got his pay, he'd go grocery shopping and take it home to his family. He'd give his sister money for school and give his mother whatever extra he had. He even teamed up with his mother and moved his family into a nicer house. The rent was a bit pricy but his mother was in love with the house when they went to the viewing and he wanted her to have it.

For her birthday he bough her a big fridge freezer like the one that she had on hire purchase, that was taken back by the company due to non-payment years earlier. His mother was elated. She'd changed how she treated him. She was much nicer; even washed his clothes on the weekends, something she'd not done since he was about 10 years old. He tried to help out his family as much as possible. At only 16 years old, he paid for his sister to take eight CXC subjects and paid for her graduation and prom. He doted on her. He knew she was smart and wanted her to have the chance he didn't have. His sister was grateful.

By the time Barrington was 17, he was earning almost $20000 per week working on construction sites. Levy sat him down and explained that he needed to ensure that he saved some of his money for the days when work wasn't as frequent. He took his advice. He went to the bank and was told that they couldn't open an account for him. He went home to get his mother's help.

"Mommy, can you do me a favour please."

"Sure my baby, what do you want me to do?"

"I want you to open a bank account for me. I want to save some rainy-day money."

"Yes I'll help. When do you want me to go to the bank and how much do you want me to put?"

"I don't have much now, I only have about $5000 I can put in now but I'll give you the money every week and you put it in for me."

"Yes, I'll do that. Give me the money and I'll go tomorrow."

"They don't open on Saturday mommy, you mean Monday right?"

"Oh yes, I forgot it's Saturday tomorrow."

He handed over the $5000 to his mother. Then gave her $7000 to pay the electric and water bill. "I'll give you my share of the rent next week. I want to get it out of the way so that I can put most of my pay in the bank the following week. Oh, wait I need to give Brandy $2000, she needs to buy a text book."

"You need to stop giving Brandy your money, she's a grown woman now. She can go get a job."

"Mommy don't start please. She's doing her best. She's my sister I want to help her."

"But Barrington, she needs to go get a job or find herself a man. She can't just depend on everybody else."

"Mommy, stop. Just do the bank thing for me. Don't talk about what Brandy needs to do."

"Okay my son, no worries. I'll open the account for you."

Brandy stayed in the room she shared with Carl and listened to the conversation between the two of them. She appreciated the help she was getting from her brother but felt guilty. She thought he needed to go lead his own life and take care of himself. She worked the summer, weekends and afterschool three days per week but couldn't manage to do it all on her own. She appreciated the fact that her brother could fill the gaps she couldn't.

Later that evening, Brandy and Barrington went for a walk to the cook shop to buy Friday night's dinner.

"Why did you give mommy your money?"

"Don't worry about it man, she's going to open a bank account for me. I want to start saving."

"But why don't you open the account for yourself. You know you can't trust her."

"I can Brandy, she has money for everything now so she won't mess with the money. We are okay, there's no need for her to use the money."

"You know she'll find a reason. Why don't you just hide your money in a shoe or something? Can't Levy open the account for you?"

"Come on, she's our mother. Why would I trust a stranger with my money more than my own mother?"

"Because it's mommy Barrington. You know how she is and I don't want to see her hurt you again. You can afford to move out and go live your own life now. Levy isn't a stranger. He'll do anything to help you. I'm sure he won't steal from you."

"I can't move out. How will you guys manage? Mommy needs the help. It'll be okay man, don't worry so much."

"I have to worry. I don't know how you can forget things so easily. She doesn't mean you any good. She's only treating you well now because you can help her. But let's wait and see. Just remember that I warned you, and I don't mean it in a bad way. I'm just being realistic."

"Brandy, we are alright now man. Mommy changed. Just chill man."

Almost two years passed. Brandy was away at university on a full scholarship. Every week Barrington gave his mother money to put in his bank account. Under the advisement of his sister, he'd gotten himself a hard cover book where he kept track of the money he gave to her each week. For quite some time he hadn't totalled his accounts. Then one Saturday morning, with some time on his hand, he decided to add up everything he'd given his mother thus far. Barrington was surprised to see that he'd saved just over one million dollars. He never imagined he'd ever have that much money pass through his hands, let alone have it all at once. He was thrilled and wanted to see the money himself. He wanted the money to be associated with his own name.

The following Monday Barrington went to a credit union and opened up a new bank account for himself on his lunch break. He was going to get his mother to get the money out for him so that he could have it in his name. He was excited. Armed with his new bank book, Barrington went to his mother to talk about his plans later that evening.

"Mommy, I went to the credit union today. They allowed me to open a bank account."

"Really, that's so nice. Are you going to save in that as well?"

"Actually, I wanted you to get the money out of the one in your name and let me put it in this one. Can we go tomorrow?"

"Oh okay. No not tomorrow, I have to take time off work. I'll request the time when I go in tomorrow then let you know which day is good for me."

"Can't you go on your lunch time tomorrow?"

"I don't get enough time. Bank lines are always long and I can't get back to work late."

"Okay, let me know when you can please. I really want to get it into my account."

"Okay my son."

The following day, his mother told him that she'd called the bank and they said she needed a special appointment to get the money out. She told him that the bank said due to the amount of money in the account she couldn't just come in and get it. He believed her.

Days passed and she didn't mention the appointment or any progress on getting his money out of the bank. Brandy told her brother to ask for the bank book but his mother said she hadn't received one and she'd not taken a card for the account either. The only way for her to know how much was in the account was to go into the bank. She gave excuse after excuse as to why she couldn't go into the bank.

Two months passed and there was still no updates on the progress of getting his money out. Barrington grew worried that his sister's words had caught up with him. He waited for his mother on her lunch break one day at work. She kept delaying, pushing her lunch time back until it was almost 3pm and he knew there was no way they'd make it to the bank that day. He went home almost knowing for sure that something was awfully wrong. He waited for his mother outside the front gate.

"Mommy, is there any money in the bank?" he asked.

"What do you mean? Your money is in the bank."

"Mommy just be honest with me. I just want to know the truth. Is there anything left in the bank mommy?"

"Barrington, every week you give me your money, I go to the bank and put it into the account."

"Then why aren't you going to get my money out?"

"Because I don't have the time yet. I'll go next week."

"Okay mommy, I hear you."

As if it was faith chasing them down, the following day at work Barrington fell off the scaffolding at work and injured his back. He was admitted to the hospital for two weeks then finally sent home on bed rest. He couldn't work. Within a week of being of work, the landlord turned up to their home to get the rent, which was now almost two weeks late.

"Mommy, why didn't you pay the rent? I told you to pay it from the account."

"I did."

"What's wrong with you? Why are you lying? Why would the landlord be here asking for his rent if you paid it?"

"It's in his account. I've put it in there. He just needs to check."

"Mommy, please be honest with me is there any money at all in the bank?"

"Let me get out of this room because you're only upsetting me. I'll go to the bank to get your money tomorrow." His mother left the room.

Late in the night she returned to the room to confess to her son that the money wasn't in the bank. She made excuses that she'd owed a lot of money to a lot of people and had been paying them back. Barrington couldn't face his mother. As she told him the story, his heart sank. All his savings were gone. He had nothing left and now he was out of work too. He wasn't sure how much longer he was going to be home for. That night, Barrington called his sister, who didn't pick up. He sent her a message asking her to call him.

Barrington didn't sleep the entire night. His sister called him early the next morning.

"Hey, what's up?"

"Brandy, you okay?"

"Yeah, I'm okay. You? How is the pain now?"

"The pain is still there but I'm good man."

"Okay but why do you sound like that?"

"I'm good Brandy. How's school?"

"Stop beating around the bush. What did mommy do now? Did you get your money?" There was no response from her brother on the other end of the line. "Barrington? Talk to me. Barrington?"

"I'm here man. It's cool. I'm good."

"Barrington you need to call the police on her and get her to show you the bank account. What did she do with all that money? The money must be in the bank."

"There's no money Brandy, but I'm good. We all have to learn."

"Why do you keep letting her get away with things? She'll never stop. As soon as you get back on your feet you need to move out and leave her to figure things out on her own. And I hope you go back to work soon because I'm sure 'nice mommy' will be gone pretty soon if you can't give her any money."

Six more weeks passed, and Barrington had been out of work. His sister was right. His mother went back to being the same person she was before he started providing for his family. She stopped making him breakfast in the mornings and would wash up the dishes after she and Carl had dinner in the evenings. There was no dinner for him. She became irritable at the sight of him.

"Carl bring the clothes outside for me to wash them."

"Okay mommy, all of them?"

"No just ours."

"What about Barrington's?"

"Leave them, let the worthless good for nothing fool wash his own clothes. I can't be washing a grown man's clothes. I don't have a man."

"But mommy, he's sick."

"I'm sick too. Bring out the clothes."

"Okay mommy."

Barrington listened to his mother from his room and smiled to himself. He'd taken note of how she'd reverted back to who she used to be. He felt betrayed by her. He felt used. With rent and bills, Barrington blew through the little savings he had in his credit union account quickly. He didn't have any more money to give his mother and that made things bad for him. She asked for the rent in the morning and he told her he didn't have any money, which he didn't. Later that evening when Barrington came home, his clothes were waiting for him outside in the front yard.

Unice

From a very young age I knew I didn't want to have children. I saw nothing good in me that I had to offer to anyone. More importantly, I didn't want to be the kind of parent my mother was to me and my sister. When the doctor told me at only 29 that I was experiencing early menopause, I was relieved. There was no way I was going to be a mother. There was no opportunity for me to ruin a child's life the way my mother had and continued to ruin mine. The worst part is, even approaching 40, there is still something inside me that yearns for her love and affection, something that begs for her approval. I yearn for the kind of relationship so many of my friends have with their mothers. I think she knows this and uses it against me. Sometimes I wish I could abandon her and live a life of my own the way my brother has. No matter how hard I try though, something keeps pulling me back and I want to know that she is okay and taken care of.

TOO NORMAL

My mother had me just out of university. My father was a med student who lived on campus whom she'd fallen madly in love with. They were meant to get married but my father suddenly fell ill and died before I was born. Until I was four, she was a single parent working as a pharmacist. I don't remember these earlier years well, but I remember the birth of my brother when I was seven and my mother's wedding to his father. I was the flower girl at their wedding.

My stepfather was kind-hearted and awfully reserved. He was a typical Jamaican man in so many ways. His role was breadwinner. He never interfered with the way my mother disciplined me or got involved in housework and the so-called womanly things. On the weekends when school was out, he spent his time away from the house and returned at nights. He was somewhat non-existent when it came to our daily lives.

My mother was the one who raised and disciplined us. She was more than a no-nonsense kind of person. She was strict. My brother reckons she's the most cruel, sadistic person to walk the earth and sometimes I tend to agree.

She has a special streak of evil inside her and it seems to bring her pleasure to see other people in pain.

My earliest recollection of witnessing my mother's wicked nature dates back to my ninth birthday. My brother was still very young, and my mother had asked me to feed him some crushed Irish potatoes she'd left on the counter in the kitchen. I struggled to reach it and had to climb on a paint bucket to get it from the counter. While climbing down, I fell to the floor with the bowl in my hand. The potatoes splattered on the floor and my chin hit the tiled floor hard. The impact was so hard it split my chin open. I screamed for my mother, who came running but not to my rescue. My mother pulled me up from the floor by one arm and started thumping me in my back. I couldn't stop screaming but I also remembered being confused. I had fallen and hurt myself and I was bleeding, yet my mother was thumping me. With each thump she demanded I stopped crying, but I couldn't stop. When she finally stopped thumping me, she sent me to get a bucket and rag to clean up the mess of blood and mashed potato from the kitchen floor. To this very day, she never even looked at my chin to see how badly hurt I was. It wasn't until the following morning that my step father noticed and dressed it. I remember sobbing while I fell asleep that night. I still have a scar on my chin which didn't heal properly, because my mother didn't get it looked after by a doctor and it had festered a few times. That day was either the day my mother changed, or I must've blocked anything before then. The brutal beatings became a weekly pastime for my mother. If I didn't give her a reason to beat me, she'd make one up. I think she couldn't help herself; it gave her some kind of pleasure nothing else did.

When my brother was only three, he'd gotten to the stove and turned it on. My mother found him at the stove playing with the knobs, she picked him up, lit a match and fired the burner. She held my brother's face close to the flames.

"You're too damn rude. Being that you like fire, let me soothe your curiosity." She pushed his face closer to the flames and my brother groaned and struggled to get away from her.

I could notice this from the doorway of the kitchen, but I was scared to intervene. Seeing my mother grab my brother's hand and put it in the burning fire and hearing his painful shriek, I rushed in and grabbed him from my mother. His hand was badly burnt. My mother told my stepfather that he'd burnt himself and he believed her.

My stepfather believed anything my mother told him. My brother was drawing on the wall one morning with one of my pencils and my mother caught him. She grabbed the pencil from him then banged his head into the wall several times. He ended up with two big bruises on his fore head and a cut in the back of his head. My mother told my stepfather he'd fallen and he didn't question her. More and more he'd come home to injuries on us but it wasn't until he'd witnessed it for himself that he'd realised what was really going on.

The same year, my step-father left and took my brother with him. He came home to find my mother 'disciplining'

us. I know for a fact that neither of us had done anything at all that even warranted a bit of spanking. Before she started, I was lying on the floor with my brother teaching him to spell his name. Suddenly my mother called us into the kitchen, where she had poured cornmeal on the floor. She told me to take off the pair of pants I was wearing and told both me and my brother to kneel in it. It was the most painful thing I'd ever felt in my entire life. It felt like thousands of needles at a time piercing my skin. Poor Mario kept crying and standing up to escape it but each time my mother pushed him back down to his knees. He was so young. I imagined how much worse it felt for him. My knees couldn't take any more of it. I felt myself just go numb and it was as though my entire body gave up; I involuntarily sat back on my heels. My mother standing over us like a guard on watch, slapped me so hard across my face, I fell over.

"Get up! Kneel down!" She screamed like someone possessed.

I got up and kneeled back down in the cornmeal. I looked down to see that the cornmeal beneath my brother's knees was now red. He just kept crying and screaming.

"What's going on here," my stepfather said walking into the kitchen.

"Hector, look what these two kids are doing."

"Patsy, what do you mean what they are doing. I watched you outside the window Patsy. Why are you doing this to them? Are you mad? What's wrong with your head?" he picked us up from the ground.

I could barely stand up. Mario was clinging to his father's leg.

"Don't come in here all high and mighty acting as if you're the boss of me. As a matter of fact, put them back to kneel down. They need punishment."

"Punishment for what? What could two little babies do for you to do this to them? You just act crazy all the time."

My mother took up the knife and attacked my stepfather. I screamed just in time for him to turn and stop her from stabbing him. He wrestled the knife away from her. My mother started throwing the drinking glasses and plates at him. My stepfather finally escaped to our bedroom, where he packed up some of our clothes in a bag. He carried my brother and held my hand. The bag he packed was on his back. He released my hand to open the front door. My mother heard him opening the door and came running into the living room. She lunged at him, pushing my brother out of his hand.

"Where the hell do you think you're going with my children?"

"Relax yourself man," he gave her a light push to get off him. "Unice come. Take Mario and come."

"Unice if you move from over there, I'll kill you!"

"What's really wrong with you woman? Why are you so cantankerous? Get off me man."

"You're not going anywhere with my children tonight."

"They're not staying here with you. Everyday something else is wrong with them. I'm sure you're the one hurting them. Unice did you really fall when you broke your hand?"

I didn't answer. I was too scared.

"Look at that, you put so much fear in the kids. I'm not sleeping here tonight, and neither are they." He walked over and picked up Mario.

"You're not taking them anywhere. You're welcomed to go because you're just a waste man I don't need but they will not leave this house tonight or any other night."

My stepfather walked over to me and took my hand, "move out of the way so that I can leave. You need to control yourself." We moved towards the door, which my mother was blocking.

"You know what, give me my pickney," she started pulling me and I held on tight to my stepfather, who kept pulling me back.

"Patsy, leave the child alone man, you're going to hurt her if you keep pulling her like that."

"I gave birth to her, I can do whatever I want with her. Unice come."

My father opened the door and put my brother outside on the veranda. He pulled me from my mother and picked me up. My mother held on to him, trying to keep him inside the house. I buried my face in my stepfather's chest. My mother wouldn't stop pulling him and he kept trying to get out of the house. Then all of a sudden, my mother began screaming.

"Help! Help! Rape, somebody help! Call the police." She began crying and screaming as though someone was attacking her.

A man going up the road stopped to see what was going on, "Hector, everything alright man?"

"Yes Bunny, don't mind her."

"Bunny call the police please. Hector molested my child now he's trying to take her."

"Yow Hector, I'm coming into the yard. Call the dog off."

A crowd was being drawn outside our gate. "Patsy, you alright?" a voice called out from the gate.

"Bunny, come help me please."

"Patsy, I can't get pass the dog. Call him off."

"Tiger, come." Patsy called out to the dog, but he was now at the gate agitated by the crowd being drawn. "Tiger," she called out again, but the dog continued to bark at the by standers.

"If you walk out that door with Unice I swear I'm going to tell the police you raped her. Put down my pickney! Mario, come into the house."

I held on to my stepfather's neck almost stifling him. I wrapped my legs around him and wouldn't let go.

"This look strange man. How can she say the man is hurting the child but the child is holding on like she wants to go with him? This look strange."

"Tony?"

"Yes Hector. It's me man. What's going on?"

"Tony, my keys are in the car. I'm going to send the kids to you and you put them in the car for me."

"Alright brother, send them."

"Don't get involved. Don't help him take the woman's children. Either of you know baby pain. Call the police and let them figure it out themselves," my neighbour Judith said.

"Judith this woman is going to kill these kids. Call the police if you want but I'm not leaving them here."

"That's your problem you Judith, you like talking shit. This man never raised his voice ever. If the man is taking the kids there must be a problem. Help the man." Tony said.

"Tony please man. Put them in the car for me. This is only stressing them out. Anyone can pick up their phone to call the police but they really need to get away from this. I'll stay inside until the police comes.

"Tony don't touch my children. I'll tell the police the two of you are in cahoots. Leave my business alone."

"Same damn thing. Listen how she's quick to say Tony is also molesting her children. What a wicked woman?" Poochie added, "Hector send the kids, I'll put them in the car."

My stepfather tried to put me down on the veranda but I couldn't let go off his neck. "Unice, you need to let go," he tried to open the lock I had around his neck. "Come on you have to be a big sister now, go take your brother to the car. Sit in the car I'll come soon."

"Unice don't go. Hector, I swear I'll stab you right in your heart if you send my children outside!"

"Hey mad woman, leave the damn man alone. Somebody shut up this damn dog and let me go in and take them out." Judith said.

"You whoring bitch, do you think I don't know that you want my husband. If you touch any of my children, I'll kill you."

"You're free to say anything in your house but keep it in there because I'm not Hector, I won't hesitate to fuck you up."

"Judith just help me and relax, we can't be doing this around the kids." I felt his tears fall on my arm. "Unice you really have to go to the car. I promise I'm going to come. Go help your brother. He'll stop crying if you're with him."

I released my step father, climbed down and took my brother into the yard. Tiger started sniffing us and the noise calmed down. My mother kept calling me but I didn't look back for fear that she'd get me. They couldn't open the gate for fear that the dog would come out. Tony and Bunny lifted Mario over the wall first, then me.

"Look at their knees. They are bleeding," someone said.

"Yes, look." Judith bent to inspect our knees. "Unice, what happened to your knees."

I didn't answer.

"Mommy put us in cornmeal," Mario said.

"Oh my God what a wicked woman. The baby wouldn't tell a lie like that," said a man whose name I didn't know.

No one could get into the yard. I watched from inside the car as they all looked over the wall at what was unfolding. I couldn't see from inside the car. It went on for quite some time, then suddenly the gate was opened and everyone rushed into the yard. I unlocked the door and jumped out of the car. Running into the yard, I could see my stepfather lying on the ground. There was blood everywhere. I remember screaming and throwing my body on him just howling. My mother was being held down on the ground by three men as she tried to wrestle away from them.

My stepfather was stabbed in his neck while walking out of the yard but he survived. He won custody of my brother, but I had to stay with my mother and continued to endure the trauma throughout the years. My brother never speaks with her and hates the fact that I even have a relationship with her after everything I have had to endure.

When I was 34, I was outside the gate talking to a guy I was dating. My mother called me; because I didn't go immediately, she came out to the gate, told the man off and started to cuss me calling me all sorts of names. When I told her to stop disgracing me, my mother doubled her fist and punched me in my face. I was humiliated but I'd grown used to that kind of behaviour.

TOO NORMAL

Now that she has arthritis and can't do anything for herself, I'm the only one she can depend on.

Shamar and Shan

"Karen leave the pickney alone man! Everyday is the same thing," she came into the yard trying to rescue Shamar.

"Blackie, leave me alone! I'm going to kill him. Am tired of this boy, God knows am tired," she wielded the machete again, almost hitting Blackie who was now hiding Shamar behind her.

"No man, you can't beat him like this man. Put down the machete."

"Blackie, leave, me, alone. Give him to me. You help me feel pain for him? I brought him into this world and God see and know I'm sending him right back today."

"Stop the foolishness man. You want to go to prison?"

"Don't tell me about no prison. Every day this boy give me headache and problems. Am tired! Blackie, give me my pickney."

Blackie's common law husband was now behind her trying to rescue Shamar. It was their typical rescue mission when Karen was attacking any of her four children. However, they spent more time rescuing Shamar who seemed to always be doing something for Karen to beat him mercilessly. They had two kids of their own and couldn't understand why Karen needed to beat hers the way she did. She used whatever was in her reach to beat them and today she was using a machete to beat Shamar. The boy was already bruised from head to toe, most of his scars a result of his mother's beating.

At 15, Shamar was a good Jamaican boy child. He never got into trouble, went to school everyday even without money, went to church on Sundays and was liked by all his neighbours. They all thought he was growing into a wonderful young man. Karen, they all agreed, simply took out her problems on the children. She was nice and jolly when there was a man in her life taking care of her, but the moment they left, her anger would turn to the kids.

That Sunday afternoon she was about to kill poor Shamar because he came home from church and was still in his church clothes after her telling him to take it off twice. He was busy playing with his little sister when she attacked him.

"Michael, leave Shamar alone, leave him alone and move!" she screamed.

"Karen, just calm down, there's no reason to beat him like this man. Nobody is saying you shouldn't discipline the young man, but this is taking it too far. You must stop this now man."

"Who the hell do you think you are? Don't tell me how to run my house! As a matter of fact, get out of my yard! Come out!"

"Fine, come Shamar."

"Wait, 'come Shamar', come where? If Shamar leave this yard, I kill him!"

"Shan, bring some water for your mother." Blackie motioned to the oldest child stood crying not even a metre away from her mother. She didn't move. "Shan?" Blackie called out to her, but she appeared to be in a daze.

"Karen," came a call from across the fence on the opposite side of her house.

"Teddy don't call my name. All of you leave me alone and let me do what I want with my pickney, not one of you help me feed or clothes them. I will do as I please. I brought all four of them into the world and I can take them out if I want to. Not one of you can stop me from beating Shamar today, not one of you! Shamar go into the house now and don't let me have to tell you again."

A shaking Shamar tried to pull away from Michael, but he held on to him. "He's not going into the house. Put down the machete and go calm down, then he'll come back over later. He's bleeding so that needs to be looked after."

Blackie tried to take the machete, but she held on to it for dear life.

"Mommy, put down the machete," Shan finally spoke.

She walked over to her mother, Blackie's fingers locked around her trying to pry the machete out of her hand. Shan held onto the machete and her mother finally released it. As she had done with many of the objects her mother had previously used to beat them, she walked out of the yard with the machete, through the streets and eventually down to the gutter to dump the machete. She knew when her mother was ready to use the machete and couldn't find it, they would probably all be in trouble but for now she wanted to get rid of the object that her mother was using to beat her brother. Inside she was angry, she wanted to stop her mother but didn't know how, and while Blackie and Michael were trying to rescue Shamar, the only thing going through her mind was taking the machete from her mother and beating her with it. She wanted her to feel the same pain she was inflicting on him.

For the rest of the day Shamar was away being looked after by the neighbours and his older sister was left to deal with the backlash of her mother's unreleased anger. Shan was preparing for CXCs, her third exam was coming up the following Tuesday and she wanted to be ready. She had already made up her mind that she would make sure to pass all her subjects so she could get a job and move out of the house, taking her brother with her. The two younger children were beaten but never like the two of them. Shan knew how to avoid her mother, stay out of her way. She wasn't always successful but her tactics helped massively. She knew what her mother liked and disliked. She knew the triggers. Whenever, she noticed that the latest boyfriend wasn't coming around, she implemented all her precautionary measures. She resented her mother too. Years earlier, she had told her mother that her youngest sister's father was molesting her; her mother never believed her. He ran away when Shan said she was going to tell the police and neither the kids nor Karen had seen him since.

Late in the evening when it was time for bed, Blackie walked Shamar home.

"You okay now?" she asked Karen.

"Don't I look okay?"

"Hm, I hope so. Remember he has school tomorrow and he's full of cuts so let him sleep in peace."

"Blackie, why are you always trying to tell me what to do in my house?"

"I'm not telling you what to do in your house. Anyway he ate dinner already. I'm going now, I don't want to upset you."

"Upset me? You can't upset me."

"Good night Karen."

Shamar was already in bed. He had quickly gotten into the house and 'gotten out of his mother's way'.

"Shamar," Karen called out.

"He's sleeping mommy," the youngest of the four children responded.

"Tell Shamar to come here and don't get me mad. He can't be sleeping already."

"Yes mommy," Shamar presented himself promptly.

"Come here let me see the cuts." Shamar came close and his mother inspected him. Fear lingered inside him, but his mother had sounded much calmer, so he thought she was sincere in seeing what she'd done to him. She looked at the scars on his hands, shoulders and back. "Go to your bed," she instructed him.

Shamar turned to walk back to his room. His mother picked up the large dolphin figurine nearest her on the what-not and threw it with all her might at Shamar. He had no time to move out of the way, his back was turned, and the figurine hit him in the back of his head.

"Woi!" Shamar shrieked, grabbing the back of his head. Blood gushed from it.

Shan heard his scream and came running.

"Shan lend me $1000, I'll pay you back tomorrow."

"Mommy I only have my fare for work for the week. I know you won't give it back and I can't afford to miss work."

"Ungrateful john crow. Dog shit, you expect to live here without helping? As a matter of fact, you're right you won't get it back. Give me the $1000 and now too." Things escalated quickly.

"Mommy I can't give you the money." Shan was holding her ground. She'd been working for eight months and hadn't been able to save a cent. She wanted to move out but couldn't save because of her mother. If Shan left money in her handbag, her mother would steal it then fight with Shan about the money to not give her back. Shan had to bury her money in the yard in order to hold on to any of it to get to and from work each day. On top of stealing her money, her mother collected rent from her. Shan had to pay half the rent and electric bill and the full water rates, plus give her siblings money for school, which meant she barely had any money left for herself. She didn't have enough to last for food and travelling each week.

"Shamar bring Shan's handbag to me."

Knowing full well that Shan didn't have the money in her handbag, Shamar brought the bag to his mother. "Here mommy," he handed it to her.

She searched through the bag but couldn't find the money, "did you hide it? Shan, I need the money so we can have dinner later. Stop messing about and give me the money."

"Mommy there's food in the house. I don't have any money."

"Stop talking shit! I don't want what's in the house. I want to cook chicken tomorrow. You have money. How will you get to work tomorrow morning then?"

"I already paid the driver."

"Shan you're really not going to give me the money?"

"I don't have any money." Shan said.

"You ungrateful wretch. It's fine Shan, keep your money. I hope it lasts."

Shan didn't respond. She knew her mother didn't believe her about paying the driver. She also knew there was chicken in the freezer; that her mother was conning her. Later in the night when she heard her mother snoring, Shan asked Shamar to go dig up a spot to take money out for the two of them. She hid her share of the money in her shoes and Shamar hid his in his book. The kids went to bed.

The next morning Shan searched her shoes for her $400 frantically. She knew for a fact that she'd put it in the left foot as she always did. She pushed her finger into the toe of the shoes digging, hoping by some miracle the money was too far in. She banged the shoes on the floor trying to shake money out of it. She did the same to the right foot too but there was no money falling out. Shan searched her other pair of work shoes, then her pants pockets and all the compartments of her handbag. She couldn't find the money anywhere.

"What are you looking for?"

"I can't find my money. Did you see where I put it last night?"

"It's in your black shoes."

"Shamar, it's not there. It's not in any of them. I can't find it anywhere."

"Maybe it fell out under the bed when you were taking it out. Let me help you look for it." Shamar bent down to search for the money.

Shan searched the pillow case and under the sheets of the bed she'd only just made up. She could hear her mother humming in her room. She patted Shamar on his back and signalled to him to stand up.

"Did you check for your money this morning?"

"No," Shamar grabbed his bag and pulled out his book shaking it on the bed. The money wasn't falling out.

"Maybe it's not that book. Let me help you look."

The two of them searched all the books looking for the money but they couldn't find it. It was gone. Both their stashes had been stolen. They were sure that they hadn't miss placed it. The two of them looked at each other at the same time, realising that their mother had taken their money. Shan got up from the bed and Shamar grabbed her hand trying to hold her back. She pulled away from him and walked out the room.

"Mommy," she knocked on her mother's door. "Mommy?" Her mother didn't answer. Shan turned the lock trying to open the door.

"Who's opening my door?"

"Mommy, it's me."

"Me who?"

"Mommy open the door please."

"Move away from my door. Aren't you going to work?"

"I need my money."

"Which money? Didn't you pay the driver already?"

"The money you took from my shoes and Shamar's book." Shan banged on the door.

"If you knock on my door one more time you won't like it. You didn't have any money so I didn't take any money."

"Mommy I need to go to work. Can I have my money please?"

"Shithouse, stop accusing me. How can you lose money you didn't have? Move from my door."

"Mommy, please give me back the money. I have to go to work and Shamar is late for school."

"Shan, you and Shamar didn't have any money last night so how could you lose money this morning?"

"Mommy can I have my money please?"

Shan heard her mother's footsteps coming towards the door and stepped back. Her mother appeared in the door way, inspecting her nails as though all was right in the world. She spread her fingers, viewing her nails from another angle.

"What is your problem?"

"I need my money."

"Which money?"

"You know which money I'm talking about. I need my money to go to work and Shamar needs his money for school."

"Who has your money?"

"Mommy can you stop and just give back the money please?"

"Shan, if you ask me for that money one more time, you won't like it. Go and wait for the driver that you paid to take you to work."

All this while Shamar had been outside digging up another stash of Shan's money. He walked into the living room with his sister's shoes and handbag.

"Shan come, let's see if we can figure something out together."

"Shamar, I need my money."

"Just come Shan."

"You better listen to your brother and go before you get something to regret." She went back into her room, slamming the door.

She pressed her foot down on his neck harder. He held on to her ankle trying to pull her off him but couldn't. He was choking. Shamar's eyes, bloodshot red, spewed tears down his temple. He couldn't speak. She pressed harder. She lifted her foot up for a brief second and then stepped on the side of his face, pushing his head into the floor. As soon as he stopped fighting, she stepped off him and went outside. Shamar flew into a fit, coughing uncontrollably; his spit drooling to the floor and mixing with his tears. He saw his mother coming back. He got up and ran towards the front door but couldn't open it quickly enough. She started beating him with the electrical wire across his back. He felt the cord rip through his flesh. He tried to climb through the locked door to escape his mother. He turned around, throwing his hand up trying to grab hold of the wire. His thumb got caught in it and his mother pulled the wire back to her, pulling his finger so hard it bent back towards his wrist. Shamar tried to run past his mother and she threw him to the floor with a hook. She kneeled on him and wrapped the cord around his neck.

"I'll kill you you know Shamar. You want to fight me? Hm?" She wrapped the cord around his neck tighter, pulling him up towards her. His eyes were pulping out. "You think you're a man, so I'll treat you like a man." She pulled on the cord even tighter. Shamar tried to cough but the cord was too tight around his neck His eyes kept bulging out and he tried to loosen the cord around his neck without any success.

"Mommy," it came out like a squeaky inaudible whisper.

His mother removed her right hand from the rope, pulling it tight still, with only her left. She used her thumb and index finger to squeeze his nose, cutting off the air. Shamar, unable to breathe, started kicking violently, throwing his mother on her back on the floor next to him. He loosened the cord from around his neck, got up from the floor, and ran out the back door. He was stark naked.

Shamar just came out of the shower and stood in his room trying to get dressed. He didn't have money for school, so he'd stayed home. For transportation alone, it was almost $600 per day for school. Shan couldn't help her brother that morning because she didn't have enough. Since she's started working, her mother had stopped giving Shamar money to go to school all together. That Friday morning, she didn't have enough for the two of them so she told her brother to stay home.

"Why are you still at home," she'd asked.

"I'm not going to school today, I don't have any money."

"What do you mean, didn't your sister give you money."

"She didn't have any."

"Shan always have money, she's too fucking mean."

"Mommy if she had it she would have given me. She doesn't even have money to come home."

"Stop taking her side. Sometimes you act as if you're fucking your sister."

Shamar sighed at his mother's remark, "I still have time to get to school on time. Don't you have any money?"

"I don't have any money."

"Yeah, so Shan don't have any either. She doesn't have a tree to pick money from."

"What did you say?"

"Nothing mommy."

"Where does Shan hide her money? I know that you know. Tell me and I'll split it with you."

"You always tell us not to steal but you can afford to steal from your own children." He shook his head in contempt.

"Don't get familiar with me. It's not stealing. You guys expect to live off me and not give me anything? You think

I'm a charity? As soon as you start working you will pay me back too. All of you will. There's no place any of you can hide money in this house and expect me not to find it. I'm not taking care of no adults. I've done enough for all of you. You need to do your bit too. Shan needs to do her bit and so will you too. I can't send you all the way through high school, let you get qualification and then not profit from it."

"Mommy, you haven't helped me to go to school. If it wasn't for Shan I wouldn't be gong at all."

"Who do you think you're talking to?"

"I need to put on my clothes please. Can you close the door so I can get dressed please?"

"Close which door? That's the problem you think you're too big." She lunged at Shamar on the bed.

The assault then led into the living room and continued in the yard. That day Shamar ended up running down the street naked, trying to escape his mother. Humiliated.

Ericka

"Shevon wake up Ericka and tell her to come here for me."

"Mammy, the room is right there, just call him yourself." The annoyed 10 years old boy turned his attention back to his phone.

Sonia hissed her teeth then called out for her niece who was already busy sorting the clothes to handwash the entire family's week's worth of clothing and bedding. Before that, she had stripped the four beds in the house at her aunt's request and had cleaned the house top to bottom; washed the dishes, cleaned the kitchen, cleaned the two bathrooms, polished the veranda and mopped all the floors in the whole house. She had prepared breakfast too for her aunt and three cousins. Her makeshift bed on the living room floor was no longer in sight, she'd tucked it away neatly. She was now getting ready to do the washing but then her aunt summoned her.

"Ericka!" she paused for a moment, "Ericka!" she called out louder.

"Yes aunty," Ericka stood in the doorway of the living room, waiting to hear why her aunt had called her.

"Pass me the remote."

The girl had to go past her aunt to pick up the remote sat on the sofa next to her. Her two younger children sat in either single seated sofa next to her.

"Ericka bring me some of the lemonade in the fridge," Shevon said.

"And bring me a banana chips," his younger sister Lala added.

Ericka turned to fulfil their orders, but her aunt stopped her, "when will you start the washing? It looks like it's going to rain so you need to hurry up."

"I'm going now aunty, as soon as I finish this," she replied.

Ericka was busy outside filling the basins with water to soak the whites to get rid of the stains, while she washed the rest of the clothes. She's not even managed to get the laundry out into the yard yet, when her aunt called her again to remind her it's lunch time and she needed to prepare lunch for the family. She paused the washing and prepared them corned beef sandwiches, which was the typical Saturday lunch. Her lunch though, was the remainder of what the family didn't or couldn't eat.

Finally, just before the sun went down Ericka hung up the last set of washing. She washed the basins she'd done the washing in, swept up the yard, had a bath in her little pale and changed into her dry dress. She washed the panty and other dress she took off and hung it on the short line further towards the back of the yard. She wasn't allowed to wash her clothes with the family's or hang her clothes on the lines used to hang there's. Even when they were empty, she wasn't allowed to use them.

Ericka came inside and sat on the floor next to the sofa Shevon was sitting in. Shevon swung his foot over the side of the chair, kicking her in her head.

"Shevon, can't you say sorry. You kicked me in my head."

"But why are you sitting there. Sit over there," he pointed to the kitchen.

"I want to watch the TV. Why did you put your foot here all of a sudden?"

"Because I don't want you to sit near me."

Shevon started kicking both legs, kicking Ericka in her face.

"Aunty, can you tell Shevon to stop it please."

"Let him sit how he wants to sit. Move from beside his chair."

"But Aunty, I just want to watch the TV. Where else can I sit? You said I mustn't sit on your furniture."

"And I still don't want you sitting on them but you can't sit in his way. Did you do the ironing already?"

"Aunty, I'm planning to iron everything tomorrow because the uniforms are on the line."

"Find something do. As a matter of fact, I don't think I'm in the mood to cook tonight. Put back the things in the fridge and I'll cook the soup on Wednesday. Put on some rice and mackerel."

"Mommy I don't want that. We ate mackerel this morning." Lala said.

"Then what do you want?"

"I want chicken, chicken with mac and cheese."

"I feel for the rice and mackerel so make that for me and Shevon and fry two chicken leg for her and make the mac and cheese for her."

"I don't want mackerel either. I want chicken but not the mac and cheese."

"What will you eat the chicken with?"

"Hm," he paused to think, "dumplings."

"Everybody wants something different. I should just make the soup. But, no. I'm too tired. Ericka just make what they want and make the mackerel and rice for me."

Ericka was exhausted. She'd been up since before dawn, on her feet all day. She had barely eaten. The thought of making the food felt like torture. She'd have to drool over the food in hope that she'd get some leftovers but almost sure that she wouldn't. Then it dawned on her, that she could add a bit more to every dish she was preparing than any of them could eat to ensure that there'd be some leftovers for her. The thought got her through the cooking. She was even more pleased that her tactics had worked. While washing up the dishes, Ericka scuffed all the food in the pots, filling her belly. Washing up wasn't so painful that night.

When Ericka was only seven years old her aunt convinced her mother to let her move in with her. Her mother was an uneducated woman, with four other children struggling to make ends meet. Initially she thought she'd get the help she needed by having Ericka's aunt take her off her hand for a while, but one month turned into two then into three years. When Ericka was 10 years old, her mother passed away giving birth to her seventh child. The other children were shipped off to relatives and children's homes and

Ericka's aunt decided to keep her. There was no funeral for her mother. No one claimed the body from the hospital and no one ever told Ericka what happened to her. All she knows is that her mother died during child birth. Ericka's father was her aunt's brother, who was very much alive but took no interest in Ericka whatsoever. He led a life of his own which did not include any traces of her. He knew where she lived but that was pretty much it.

The same year she moved to live with her aunt was the same year Ericka had stopped going to school. Although her mother never had much, she'd walk Ericka and her sister, who was a year younger, to school in the morning then would walk back at lunch time to give them whatever she could find for their lunch, then be there to pick them back up after school. Moving in with her aunt was different. She had to grow up real fast. Her first order of business when she'd moved in was learning how to take care of her two cousins. Her aunt stopped sending Lala to day-care and she became Ericka's responsibility. In the afternoons before her aunt got home from work, Ericka at only seven, would have to take care of two children all on her own.

She was used to helping her mother but she'd never had to take on so much responsibilities. Ericka often think about the life she had with her mother and misses it immensely. They were dirt poor. They lived in a one-bedroom board house. The roof leaked so bad her mother would have to wait up during the nights it rained to make sure she could empty buckets before the water spilled on to the floor. They only had one bed which all five kids slept on, while their mother slept on the floor next to them. They didn't really have much but they had each other and their mother did everything she could to make sure they were okay.

Ericka can't remember ever being hungry or without food while living with her mother. In a little patch in their backyard, their mother planted cabbage, tomatoes, pumpkin, watermelon, escallion, peas, Irish potato and bananas. She always made sure she had food for them. There was always a chance it wasn't much, but they all had three meals per day. On Saturdays and Sundays they were sure they would get meat, no matter how small the amount was. Their mother worked as a 'day's worker', doing laundry for customers on Saturdays and Sunday mornings.

She was always home by lunch time to look after them. The most Ericka would ever have to do was wash her socks and panties on Saturdays and pass tools to her mother while she did the gardening. She was living out her childhood playing house with her siblings, climbing trees, playing marbles and cooking dirt and leaves. Before moving in with her aunt, Ericka was happy.

Her mother never knew what she was going through at her aunt's house. She assumed Ericka was okay; better off even. She wanted to see her more, but it wasn't possible. She feared leaving the younger ones at home alone to go see her and couldn't afford the taxi fare to pay the way for all of them. Whenever she saw her daughter, which was very rare, her aunt would never leave them alone which at the time she didn't think meant anything. When she mentioned how underweight Ericka was, Ericka's aunt would also tell her it's because she's growing. She assured her she ate like a horse and was well fed and due to how much Ericka would scuff down while visiting, she assumed it was true.

The first time Ericka visited her mother with her aunt, she cried and told her mother she wanted to stay. Her mother explained to her that it was necessary for her to be with her aunt because she didn't have enough and Ericka had reluctantly gone back with her aunt. The evening they got home, her aunt had beaten her and threatened not to take her back to see her mother if she ever cried or refused to go home with her again.

She missed her family. She was better off with her mother and her brothers and sisters. She missed playing with them, missed a nice hot meal, missed sleeping in a bed; she missed her old life. Her mother thought she was going to the same private school as her cousins. She died not knowing the truth about her daughter's life.

"Ericka come, I'm going to work now."

"Coming aunty." Ericka tried to use the toilet quickly before going into her aunt's room and crawling into the closet. She pulled her knees to her chest to sit more comfortably, resting her forehead on her knees. She heard the key turn in the door and her aunt's footsteps became more distant.

Just over a year earlier when Ericka was almost 11, a neighbour who'd just moved in had seen her outside and had called her to the fence.

"Little girl. What's your name?"

"Ericka Miss."

"That's a nice name. Are you okay?"

"Yes Miss."

"Why is your hair like that? Where is your mother?"

"My mother is dead Miss," she said hanging her head.

"Sorry Ericka, and where is your father?"

"I don't know Miss. He doesn't come to see me."

"So who do you live with here?"

"My Aunty Miss."

"Stop saying Miss. Where is your aunty?"

"Okay Miss, sorry. She's at work. She'll be home later."

"So you went to school with you hair like that?"

"I don't go to school Miss."

"What do you mean?"

"Ericka, I'm going to tell mommy you're talking to strangers." Lala yelled from the doorway.

"Bye Miss," Ericka hurried inside. She closed the door behind her and watched her neighbour's inquisitive, puzzled eyes scan every corner of the yard. She wanted to go back out and speak with her but knew she'd be in trouble when Lala told her aunt. She watched until her neighbour was gone then continued with her day.

Later that evening, she saw her aunt outside the gate talking with the same neighbour. She could tell she was angry when she came into the house, but she said nothing. The following morning her aunt locked her in her closet and left her there until she got home. The kids didn't come home that afternoon to be looked after by Ericka, they came home with their mother in the evening. Since that morning it became routine. Every morning she'd have to wake up, prepare their breakfast, bathe Lala and dress her for school, make all their beds, wash the dishes then crawl into her aunt's closet where she had no access to the toilet or anything at all. Then in the evenings, she'd be let out to continue with her chores then be able to go to bed once they'd all nodded off. At nights the doors would be locked, and her aunt would keep the keys in her room.

One weekend her aunt and the two kids went away. She didn't say where they were going or how long they'd be gone. She locked Ericka in the closet with not even as much as a glass of water early Saturday morning and left. On Sunday afternoon when they got home, Ericka was found in her mess.

"What's that smell?" Her aunt questioned, walking into her bedroom.

Ericka began to tremble. She pushed herself back on the wall of the closet, covering her face with her hands. Ashamed that she'd messed on herself.

"Ericka, did you shit in the closet?" Her aunt pulled her out of the closet.

"No aunty." She couldn't stop shaking.

"What do you mean no? What's that smell?" She spun Ericka around and lifted her dress.

"Aunty I couldn't hold it any longer. Sorry Aunty."

"Sorry? The entire damn house stinks! You're too damn disgusting! Go outside and bathe yourself then come and clean up the place. You stink!"

"Move Lala: don't let her touch you," Shevon scorned.

The faeces was stuck to her in her panties. She hung her head in shame, walking through the house to get to the backyard.

"Aunty the door is locked. I can't get out."

"Don't call me man. Damn nasty shit house! Come get the key to open the door."

"Me? No mommy. I don't want her near me. Open it yourself."

"Shevon, stop the foolishness. Come get the keys."

"Nope. Open it yourself."

She hissed her teeth then went to open the door. Ericka exited the house into the backyard. She looked around to see whether anyone was watching. With no one in sight, she filled up the basin. She took her panty off, disposing of the faeces in the outdoor toilet then washing her panties. She struggled to get the stain and the smell out of her underwear. Her aunt rushed her through bathing herself to clean the house. She emptied her closet and sent Ericka outside to wash them. Ericka was weak, she struggled to get through the washing, feeling as though she was passing out.

She quarrelled to herself the entire afternoon into the night.

At 16, Ericka was still living with her aunt and the conditions had pretty much worsened with her cousin Shevon getting older. He became more a nightmare than his mother was. By then she'd learned to steal food; just enough to get by on without her aunt knowing. She was merely skin and bones, barely weighing 90 pounds. Still she worked from morning to night at her aunt's every beck and call. While her aunt went to work, she was locked in the closet the same way she were for years. Ericka knew she didn't have many options but she'd grown tired of the life she was living. She grew tired of the closet, the hunger, being treated like a slave, everything. She began to think about a way out. She didn't care where she would end up, she just knew she wanted to escape. She wanted to get away.

One Saturday afternoon, Ericka had finished doing the laundry and filled up her basin to bathe. She saw Shevon coming outside and covered herself from him.

"What are you hiding? Do you have anything to hide?"

"I want to bathe, go back inside."

"Bathe then. I'm not watching you. You look like dead dog, no one wants to look at you."

"Aunty?" Ericka called out.

"Yow, stop calling mommy before I use this shoe and slap you across your face."

"Aunty?"

"Why are you calling me?" Her aunt appeared in the back doorway.

"Tell Shevon to come inside please. I want to bathe."

"How is he bothering you? He's in his yard. Bathe if you want to and come in. You need to iron the church clothes for tomorrow."

"But Aunty I can't bathe with Shevon standing there."

"Yow, don't call my name."

"Ericka, bathe and come inside now or just come and do this ironing. I don't have time for this. Don't call me again."

She went back inside. Shevon walked over to where Ericka was trying to bathe, unzipped his pants, took his penis out and peed in her basin of water. She pushed him but it didn't even shift him. He zipped his pants up and reached out for her, grabbing her by the back of her neck and held her head down in the basin. She was no match for him. She felt as though she was drowning. When he released her, he bent down at the tap and washed his hands then went back into the house.

Ericka never said anything to her aunt. She'd gotten used to Shevon getting away with anything he did to her. Even if his mother saw him doing something to her she wouldn't reprimand or discipline him. If anything, it was Ericka who would be reprimanded.

One evening after her aunt and cousins had dinner, Ericka collected all their leftovers in the ice cream bowl she kept under the counter in the kitchen for herself. She packed all the dishes in the bowl to take them outside and rested her bowl of left overs on the top of the pile.

"What is this?" Shevon asked, as she was walking past him in the hallway.

"Nothing," she responded hastily.

"Are you going to eat this?"

"No, I won't."

"Don't lie I know you're going to eat it."

"I won't", she insisted.

Shevon picked up the bowl, coughed up as much as he could and spat in the bowl mixing it up with the spoon in it. "You won't mind that then." He rested the bowl back on the pile.

Everything inside Ericka tightened. She wanted to hit him. She was sure he knew she needed it. She didn't sit with them to eat dinner and there was none set aside for her. He was grown enough to know that she collected the food for herself and cruel enough to have spat in it to make sure she had nothing. Thoughts of hitting him raced through her mind and knowing there was nothing to eat, she felt weak. Her arms loosened around the basin with the dishes and the pile fell to the floor.

"What's that?" Her aunt asked, coming into the hallway where she found Shevon and Ericka.

"Aunty, why don't you just kill me or put me out on the street?"

"What is the problem? Clean up the floor and don't start with your antics. Make sure nothing broke."

"Aunty I'm hungry. I'm tired. Aunty why do you treat me like this? Why do you treat me like I'm a slave?" Ericka was crying.

"Look here, don't make any noise in my house and don't accuse me of anything. Do you know how many children wish someone would provide a roof over their heads and give them a chance? If I didn't take you from your mother you would be nothing. You'd end up just like her. A real cruff. Don't accuse me of anything; damn ungrateful! Pick up my plates and wash them."

"I wish I had turned out like my mother. I wish you didn't take me from my mother."

"Shut up, you ungrateful little bitch!" Her aunt struck her hard across her face. It even frightened Shevon, who jumped back, crashing into the wall behind him. "Pick up the dishes off my floor."

Ericka stood looking at her aunt with eyes like daggers, her heart racing and all hope of her aunt ever changing vanished from her mind.

"Pick up my things and don't let me have to tell you again." She reached out to grab Ericka, who grabbed her hand instead, pulling her down the floor. Ericka bent to the floor retrieving the dutch pot for protection but a scared Shevon ran, escaping to the living room. Her aunt lying on the floor, Ericka picked up the bowl of left overs her cousin has spat in and held her aunt down, threatening her with the dutch pot in one hand and stuffed hands full of the rice in her mouth. She coughed and choked and Erica continued to stuff her with the rice.

"My mother sent me to school. My mother fed me. My mother showed be love. Don't you ever mention my mother ever again. One day you'll have to answer to God you wicked woman."

Ericka got up and went into the living room. Lala was hiding behind Shevon who stood armed with a figurine in each hand. She went into Lala's room and picked out some of her clothes, packing them into a plastic bag. She laid down on her bed, arms and leg out stretched. She could hear her aunt choking still in the hall way. She changed into a pair of her cousin's shorts, which were too big for her, even though Lala was only 10 years old. She stared at herself in the mirror and her eyes welled up with tears. She slipped on a pair of Lala's shoes then walked out of the room and into her aunt's room.

"Get out of my house!" Her aunt screamed, "get out!"

Ericka didn't answer, she'd said all she needed to. In her mind what happened to her aunt next was up to God. She found her purse in her handbag and took out all the money in it. She searched through her drawer and found her birth certificate and immunisation book. Seeing these made her emotional. She remembered the day her aunt came to collect her at her mother's house. She remembered her mother's promise that she was going to be better off. She remembered how sad her mother was; how they all cried. She looked around the room and something inside her wanted to smash everything inside the house but she pushed the thought aside. She fought back the tears. She glanced at the deodorant on her aunt's dresser and took it up dropping it in her bag.

"I'm going now. I took all the money from your purse as my pay. I'm sure it won't cover for everything I am owed but it will do." She walked out of the front door out into the yard then through the gate. She didn't know where she was going, but she knew she just hoped wherever she'd ended up was better than the last nine years of her life.

THE END

Hello friend,

Thank you for taking the time out to read this book and share in the journey of the people who contributed their stories. By doing so, you have done so much already, but if you could be a bit kinder; I would appreciate if you could leave me an honest review on Goodreads or the platform you purchased this book on.

To continue the conversation follow me on social media or visit my website. All details are below.

Website: www.kemones-gbrown.co.uk
Goodreads: Kemone S-G Brown
Facebook: @kemonesgbrown
Mailing list: kemonesgbrown@gmail.com
Business enquiries: k.brown@kemones-gbrown.co.uk

Have you had a chance to read my other title; When Rape Becomes Acceptable, Corrective Rape in Jamaica? It's available the same place you purchased this book. Otherwise visit my website and click the "Purchase Now" button or check available stores on Goodreads.

Thanks for our support
Kemone

TAMARiND HiLL
.PRESS

www.ingramcontent.com/pod-product-compliance
Lightning Source LLC
Chambersburg PA
CBHW071153070526
44584CB00019B/2776